D0294897

Marcel Krueger is a writer, translator and editor living in Ireland, and mainly writes non-fiction about places, their history, and the journeys in between. He works as the book editor of the *Elsewhere Journal* and is the contributing editor of *Sonic Iceland*. His articles and essays have been published in the *Daily Telegraph*, the *Guardian*, *Reykjavik Grapevine*, *Süddeutsche Zeitung*, *Slow Travel Berlin*, the *Matador Network* and *CNN Travel*, amongst others. Together with Paul Sullivan he is the author of *Berlin: A Literary Guide for Travellers* (I.B.Tauris, 2016).

'*Babushka's Journey* shows the effects of the terrifying last year of World War II on the former German province of East Prussia. By reaching the past through a journey of his own, Marcel Krueger discovers the extent of this destruction and what his beloved grandmother endured when she was caught up in it. This book is a moving account of family love and the devastation of war.'

Max Egremont

'Marcel Krueger tells the compelling story of his grandmother from her life in East Prussia to her captivity in Stalin's gulag, both as voyage of discovery and through the eyes of an eyewitness. We are in his debt.'

Paul Gregory, author of *Women of the Gulag*

BABUSHKA'S JOURNEY

The Dark Road to Stalin's Wartime Camps

MARCEL KRUEGER

I.B. TAURIS
LONDON · NEW YORK

Published in 2018 by
I.B.Tauris & Co. Ltd
London • New York
www.ibtauris.com

ISBN: 978 1 78453 801 9
eISBN: 978 1 78672 384 0
ePDF: 978 1 78673 384 9

A full CIP record for this book is available from the British Library
A full CIP record is available from the Library of Congress

Library of Congress Catalog Card Number: available

Printed and bound in Sweden by ScandBook AB

Some forebear of mine was a violinist,
A horseman and thief, moreover.
Isn't that where I got my wanderlust,
Why my hair smells of wind and weather?

Swarthy, guiding my hand, is it not really him
Stealing apricots from the fruit-cart?
Curly-haired, hook-nosed, is it not his whim
That my fate is all passion and hazard?

     Marina Tsvetacva, 'Some Forebear of Mine was a Violinist'

CONTENTS

ILLUSTRATIONS

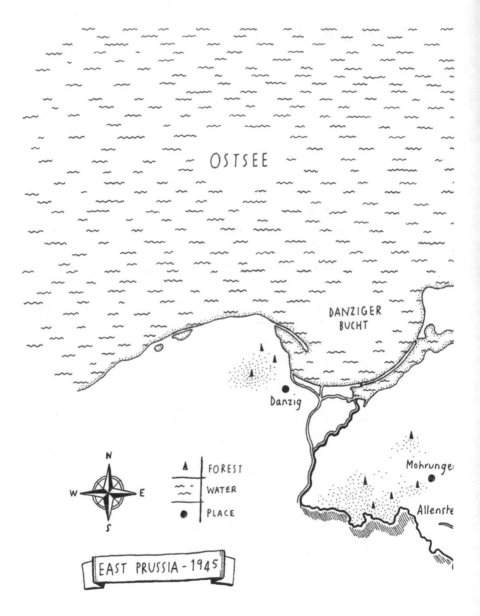

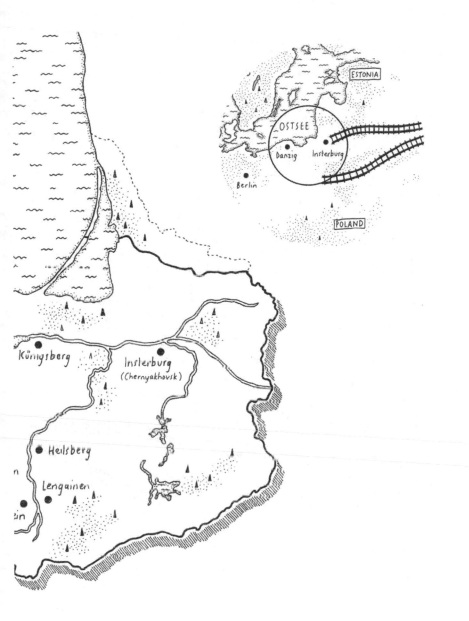

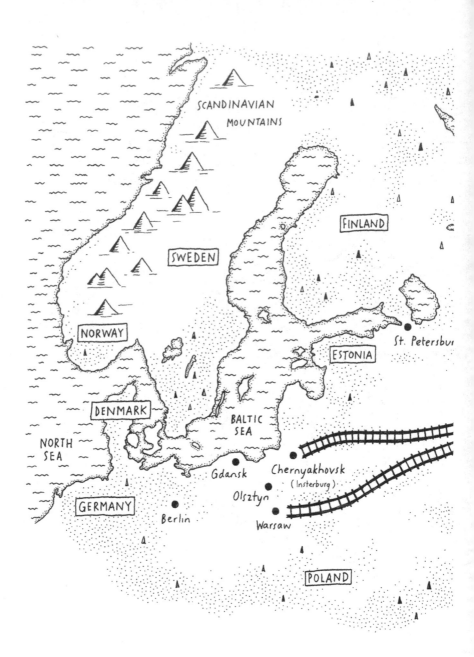

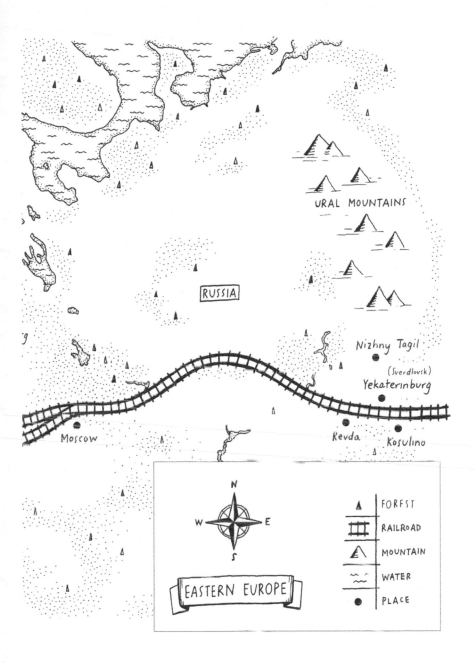

ACKNOWLEDGEMENTS

Writing a book takes a long time, longer than I had expected. Writing a book about my grandmother was confusing and sometimes painful and sometimes fantastic. This is not a thoroughly researched non-fiction book made by a scholar. I have made up many things, and moved people and events around in time and space to make them fit Cilly's story better. I am the only one to blame for any blatant mistakes, inconsistencies and typos in here.

For the real research and the shaping of a messy manuscript into something resembling a book, I am however indebted to many fantastic people. I would not have been able to do this without them. First and foremost, my editors Tatiana Wilde and Victoria Gosling as well as my copyeditors Penny Woods and Monica Guy. I will think twice about writing a book in English in the future without them.

Every travel book needs maps, and the amazing Katrin Hagen aka Mischief Champion created the ones for this book.

In Germany, the German Red Cross, Zeitzeugenbörse (Time Witness Association) in Berlin and the Friedland Museum. Luba Kemenova at ostPost berlin for her excellent translation of Cilly's file.

In Poland, the Olsztyn Tourist Office, which opened my eyes to the medieval structure of that city. Frau Barczewski and everyone at the German Minority Association, who were extremely welcoming and put me in touch with many time witnesses. Stefan Markiewicz for an eye-opening lunch where he thought I was a hipster.

In Russia, I would have been even more lost than I already

was without Luba Suslyakova, who not only told me ghost stories about my hotels but gave me gems to keep. Elenka Bobrova and Sasha Guzeva opened my eyes to the beauty of Moscow and showed me that there is some real interest among the younger Russian society in the negative aspects of Stalinism. Alexey Subbotin for buying me Guinness and helping with the train ticket.

My time travellers: Frau Moritz in Olsztyn, Frau Petenati and Frau Arndt in Berlin, Frau Rumin in Cologne and Herr Lauser in Solingen, who not only served me gallons of coffee, cheesecake and marble cake and bread and mackerels and beer but also helped me to understand the life of my grandmother through their experiences.

My family: my father Lothar who openly shared everything about his mother with me, supported my search from day one and gave me Cilly's crucifix, and my mother Edeltraut who really helped me to understand the problematic aspects of Cilly's later life. My grand-cousin Gisela made crucial details of the family history and a wealth of images available to me, and cooked me Königsberger Klopse.

I also want to mention the music that helped me through my journey: my travels were constantly accompanied by the fantastic EP of Orkiestra Wczorajszego Fasonu from Olsztyn; and I mostly wrote Cilly's story to the soundtrack of Max Richter's album *Memoryhouse*, which somehow became the soundtrack to Cilly's journey in my head. Max also kindly permitted me to use the titles of two of his compositions as chapter titles.

Last but not at all least I'd like to thank my wife Anne, who still puts up with a husband who spends most of his time on trains and with his head in World War II. I love you.

INTRODUCTION

Graham Greene tells us that childhood is the credit balance of the writer. By that measure, I was born wealthy at least. While I had a peaceful childhood, growing up in a small town in prosperous West Germany through the last two decades of the Cold War, I never lacked excitement. From a young age I was inundated with stories, from the bedtime stories of my father to the stories I discovered between the covers of the books in the local library and the adult stories I would sometimes hear my parents and grandparents talk about, stories of war and shrapnel wounds and a large homestead in a faraway land that no longer existed. It was exciting to listen to these stories, and to keep spinning them in my head. In the end, after a degustation period of over 30 years, I decided to sit down and retell some of these stories, and explore the long-gone country myself. Sadly, the main source and the main protagonist of these stories, my grandmother Cäcilie, is no longer with us. So this book is my feeble attempt at giving shape and structure to the many stories she told me, many happy, some sad, some never mentioned to me when I was little. I tried to fill in the blanks of her stories, or those dark memories she would not part with, with fiction and facts both, and counterbalance them with stories of my own travels to Eastern Europe. One summer I went to Poland to see for the first time the land my grandmother so often spoke about, and then followed her train journey to the camps in the Urals with a journey of my own via Warsaw and Moscow.

While for me as a child, the stories from East Prussia and Russia, of potato harvests and prison camps, seemed like fairy tales, from the same realm as stories of Hobbiton and Red Riding Hood, they took place in the world. So when I went to Poland and Russia to gather material for this book, I also went to see the land, to let my mind's eye feast on it and add to the store of detail I was patiently accumulating. As I travelled, I imagined Cäcilie, or Cilly as we called her, in all the places I knew she had been before me. I saw her as a young woman growing up on a farm amidst the forests of East Prussia, as a prisoner on a train, freezing and hopeless, and as part of a group of women pushing coal trolleys in a mine in the Urals.

On my return, I wrote this book, an amalgamation of research, study, eyewitness interviews, secondary sources and witness statements. The things I write about happened, if not in Cilly's camp then in others. But there were things I could not find out: how many women she knew from home in the camps, what they talked about, what they felt. Had I expected to, as though history was a book and I could turn to the back and look up all the answers? So I have made my grandmother a character in her own story. I wove a fabric from recorded history, the stories I was told over Sunday lunch so many years ago, and the images that pursued from museums and Russian steppes at dawn, of the train tracks vanishing into the distance...

What you read here is what I have made of Cilly's snippets and my feeble attempts at filling in the blanks. I offer you these glimpses as I experienced them, so that she may live once more, however briefly. Ignorance is an occupational hazard given the scale of World War II, which brought so much misery to my grandmother and her family. The more you know, the greater the realisation that there is so much more to find out. The war remains an unending repository of buried memory, which will keep families and historians busy forever. So here is a small story from that war and its aftermath; nothing more and nothing less. This is the story of Cilly and Marcel, many decades apart.

1 BABUSHKA

The past is a foreign country: they do things differently there.

L.P. Hartley, *The Go-Between*

The young woman walks home through the fields with an empty coffee pot dangling from her right hand. She is 18 years old and no beauty, the girl from the Barabasch farm. Her shoulders are too broad, her figure too stocky. Her hair is a mess of brown-black curls, and she is wearing a faded red scarf. She has low-hanging bushy eyebrows, hazel eyes, and a large hooked nose which dominates her round face. She has rough hands, and strong arms and legs from years of farm labour. She is wearing a coarse blue dress and an apron, her shoes are wooden clogs, and there's a spring in her step. Earlier, she took a drink to her brothers in the field, but they scolded her for bringing hot coffee on a day when the sun is beating down. To placate them, she put the coffee pot in a nearby stream, and while it cooled she sat and watched the sun slowly setting over the fields, that strong summer sun that seems to linger long here in East Prussia, and only the storks leaving for the south in autumn take it with them.

Now she is walking home to her mother and her younger sister Monika in the large white farmhouse sitting on a hill amidst the fields. Cilly wonders what it would be like to travel and see the world, to take a train from Allenstein station to the places she has heard about on the radio: Berlin, Paris and Rome ... Suddenly there's a loud roaring in the sky, a dark, stuttering vibration in the air, and as she turns around she sees three aeroplanes flying low over the fields. She thinks of her young brother Bruno and how much he would love to see the planes, but she does not need him to identify them for her – she knows that these are *Sturzkampfbomber*, the so-called Stuka dive bombers from nearby Grieslinen airfield. This moment with the machines in the sky is all hers. She jumps and laughs and waves as the planes roar over her, and the leading plane seems to wiggle its wings back at her. She starts to run and follows the planes, kicking up dust as she speeds homewards, following the path of the planes towards the East. It is August 1941, and the future is golden for any German who believes the war is going well.

~

When you are little, you know next to nothing. I did not know that the world in which I lived – comfortable, predictable, in which we had pork cutlets with mash for dinner on Sundays, with second helpings if we wanted them – was not my grandmother's first world, or even her second. Those had been different places, governed by other, more primeval laws.

My grandparents lived in a small apartment in a nineteenth-century house in my hometown Solingen, with a dark stairwell which always seemed to smell of cooked cabbage. As a child, I loved walking up the old and creaking stairs, as I knew that when I reached the third-floor apartment, my grandmother would be there to smother me with kisses and sneak sweets into my pockets. My grandfather, Willy, never got up when I arrived. He was content sitting in his armchair all day, reading newspapers and watching TV, occasionally grabbing and tickling my brothers and me when we came within reach. He sometimes forayed to the large table in the dining room to peel potatoes or to fill up the oil heater in the living room, but mostly I remember him sitting in his green armchair in the living room, sometimes taking a nap like a homely old cat. My

1 The Barabasch Farm

grandmother was livelier. She usually kept busy in the kitchen, and often played with us, usually card or board games. She took me on long walks deep into the countryside, through woods and along fields to churches, monuments and cemeteries, always moving, moving. I went along for the treats she would buy me from shops along the way. Nothing too fancy though – she was always careful with money. My grandmother's name was Cäcilie, but everyone called her Cilly.

On the wall of my grandparents' dining room was a large framed charcoal drawing of a farm building with two dark barns attached to it. In the picture, the farm sat atop a small hill against a background of low-hanging clouds. The drawing was black and white, a copy of a smaller black-and-white photograph that was kept stuck into the bottom of the frame. I don't remember the first time I asked about the picture, but I remember asking about it often. Depending on who was sitting around the dining room table, the answers varied, but all agreed that this was the farm that had belonged to my great-grandparents in East Prussia. It was the farm on which my grandmother grew up and which had to be left behind when the Russians came. I did not question this. As a boy growing up in West Germany in the 1980s, I knew that the Russians could come any day. Air-raid sirens howled every month, a drill preparing us for a possible nuclear attack from behind the Iron Curtain.

My grandmother often spoke of the farm, and I remember some stories more vividly than others: bringing her brothers coffee when they were working in the fields on a hot summer day; the family's dog emitting a loud howl the moment her father perished; sleigh rides through the snow to church; my grandmother frying bacon and draining the fat into a thermos filled with coffee, so her brother could weather an evening of card games and schnapps-drinking at the local pub; stories about French prisoners of war (POWs) working on the farm. I don't remember when we first talked about Russia, if my parents and grandparents sat down with us to talk about it, or if it was just another story she told one day over lunch.

But somehow, over time, it transpired that my grandmother had been captured by the Red Army at the end of the war, 'by Mongols!' as she put it, and had spent four years in camps in the Soviet Union before she came to West Germany where she met my grandfather, a former POW and fellow refugee from the East. As a child, I accepted and believed these stories in the same way that I believed fairy tales. When I heard that my grandfather had been a soldier in the war in which she was captured, I even asked if he had rescued her. I don't remember their answer.

Family stories are always prone to hyperbole and distortion, but to me the story of her capture and time in Russia felt somehow truer than others. I remember that Cilly quite openly talked about the rapes committed by soldiers in the Red Army – she did not talk about herself, but about a pregnant woman being taken to the barn, and 'all the young women that died...' Her stories were never told chronologically, always as snippets from the larger narrative: taken prisoner by the Red Army in early 1945 after they invaded East Prussia, she spent four years in Russian labour camps. She came to West Germany in 1949, and first lived with family friends in the small town of Solingen, where she met my grandfather. He also arrived there from Allied captivity and from what was Pomerania then. They married in 1952. My father was born one year later, and I arrived in 1977. Cilly died in 2009, so we had 32 years together. That was enough time for those story fragments of hers to settle and ferment in my head.

In the course of finding out more of Cilly's story, I uncovered other stories: three of my great-uncles had died during the war, one guillotined in Berlin in 1942 for spying for the Polish underground, one lost as a Wehrmacht soldier in the last days of the war, her youngest brother shot down on his first flight as a Luftwaffe fighter pilot in 1944. Scratch the world, or pick at the slightest thread, and the stories come tumbling out. The older I got the more I understood that the very fabric of the

2   Cilly and Marcel, mid-1980s

world is made of stories, and all families in Germany, Poland and Russia are related in the stories we hear and tell about World War II and its aftermath. And once you start digging, you find that even today these stories lie just under the surface of every day like hastily buried bodies, their outlines still visible.

I grew up. In my twenties I moved to Ireland, a foreign country where I knew no one and initially found it hard to understand the language. Before I found my feet, I would sometimes think of Cilly. I, at least, could always go home. I imagined sitting down to write her story from an early age, 11 or 12 maybe. But the task was daunting. All those snippets, what to do with them? And perhaps there were questions I didn't want answers to. Later, life got in the way. Cilly died in 2009 after suffering from Alzheimer's.

I never wrote down her story when she was alive, but now, after she's gone, I cannot leave it alone. It is perverse, isn't it? I tell myself that her tale should not disappear, even though her fate and that of her companions is just a small tributary to the flood of suffering that World War II brought upon everyone in Europe between 1939 and 1945. Hundreds of thousands of European citizens, mostly women, were deported to Soviet forced labour camps throughout the USSR. To this day the fate of many is unknown. But I know what happened to my grandmother, and I also want to tell her story for all those other forgotten stories. And hers is a story worth telling: a Dorothy from Nazi Germany who, plucked from her parents' farm by the tornado of war, finds herself in a strange country that tries to break and kill her. But perhaps that is not the whole of it: I have the sense that, now Cilly is dead, my curiosity cannot harm her. She is beyond harm now. Nor can she dispute my version of events, for good or ill; to tell a story we must become its author, and perhaps it is convenient to have a protagonist who can no longer protest or contradict, or turn away and say, 'I do not remember' or even, 'Why would you have me remember?'

2 KATASTROPHE

In reality, of course, history took a different term, for, whenever one
is imagining a bright future, the next catastrophe is just around the
corner.

W.G. Sebald, *Die Ringe des Saturn*

January 1945 was one of the coldest months ever recorded in
north-east Europe. At night, the temperature fell to minus 25
degrees Celsius, and by day it rarely rose above freezing. The
ground froze and the Baltic Sea was covered with a solid layer
of ice. But despite these conditions, on 13 January 1945 the Red
Army opened the final chapter of World War II in Europe: the
East Prussian Offensive. Almost 1.7 million Red Army soldiers
faced 500,000 battle-weary Wehrmacht defenders over the frozen landscape of the easternmost province of the German
Reich.

The Soviet offensive began with a heavy preparatory bom-
bardment. The one-hour barrage that preceded the attack fell
on fog-shrouded German lines, and as the fog began to clear,
smoke and dust rose into the cold sky to obscure the vision of
both attackers and defenders. But soon the Russians smashed
the measly German defence lines, and T-34 tanks and cavalry
units rushed through. Nevertheless, stubborn pockets of German resistance inflicted heavy casualties among Red Army
troops. Against this fierce resistance, Soviet General Konstan-
tin Rokossovsky launched an attack across the River Narew on
14 January; on 20 January, he received orders to swing the axis
of his advance northwards towards Elbing and the Baltic Sea.

This sudden change of direction caught the German commanders by surprise; on 22 January at 3 a.m., the 3rd Guards Cavalry Corps captured the city and district of Allenstein.

~

As I step from the Gdansk–Olsztyn train, I almost wish it were winter. While the train had been nice and airy, with the wind blowing through the half-open window in my compartment, stepping out into the festering July heat in Olsztyn is like a slap in the face. It's 32 degrees Celsius, there's no wind, and I have decided to carry my bags through town to my hotel. I could take a taxi, but I don't trust my tiny supply of Polish words to get me there, so I resort to walking. The post-modern concrete of the central station and the cracked asphalt in front of it do not suggest I am in a medieval city at all, merely another small provincial town somewhere in Poland. Prefabricated concrete high-rises, the preferred tenement buildings of Warsaw Pact countries, are everywhere, with a few old buses and dried-out parks thrown in. It smells of exhaust fumes.

In January 1945, on a platform at this station, which was then Allenstein's main station, the director of the local district court shot his wife and two children, then put a bullet in his own brain, in his fear-crazed mind saving them all from the Red Army.

My journey here was pleasant: I watched the flat landscape of Pomerania morph into the hills, blue lakes and wheat fields of Warmia-Masuria. There was the immense red-brick castle of Malbork, and dark woods filled with mossy creeks that the train seemed to glide through slowly and almost soundlessly. The day before, when I had stared out of the window of the bus that took me from Berlin to the train in Gdansk, I had seen old women with headscarves and washed-out Mickey Mouse T-shirts in front of grey and dirty crumbling high-rise estates, the River Oder squeezed into concrete banks in Szczecin, the potholes of local bus depots; everything exactly as I imagined a

3 *Postcard of Allenstein, 1931*

former Communist state would look.

From Olsztyn station, I walk down Partyzantów, the four-lane road from the train station towards Stare Miasto, the Old Town. Along the way, 1980s socialist concrete slowly gives way to older buildings and smaller tree-lined streets, and when I stop in front of the impressive neo-Gothic sandstone city hall from 1912, I see the impressive even older red-brick castle looming over the old town.

Olsztyn is the capital of the Warmia-Masuria province in north-east Poland. When my grandmother was a child, the town was called Allenstein. She grew up in a small village a few kilometres to the east, and would have come here often, to visit family members in town, on market days or for shopping trips. I do remember her mentioning *Kreis Allenstein*, Allenstein district, quite often. Allenstein was an old German city: built in 1346 as a settlement of the Teutonic Knights, it survived invasions, the bubonic plague and a brief occupation by Czarist troops during World War I. It was a beautiful town with churches and a large castle built in local red sandstone, an al-

most intact city wall and a medieval city centre with two mar-
ketplaces surrounded by nineteenth-century merchant houses.
It was only a short trip on the train or with the horse and trap
from her village of Lengainen.

Cilly was the second of four children born to my great-
grandparents, Ottilie and Johannes Barabasch. Her older sister
was named Lucie, her brother Bruno, and the youngest was her
sister Monika, born in 1933. Cilly had three half-siblings: Otto,
Franz and Otti, born to Ottilie and her first husband, Peter
Nerowski, who perished in World War I.

In a photo album I found a picture of the wedding of my
great-grandparents, a group picture with all guests, dating
from 1919. The picture must have been taken in spring or summer, as the trees behind the group are covered in leaves – but
the people frozen in black and white look like an assortment of
the German spectres that haunt East Prussia, then and now.
The picture is not yet 100 years old, but for me it might be a
copperplate engraving from the seventeenth century – that's
how strange it feels. There are almost 30 people surrounding
the sober-looking couple in the centre of the picture. My great-
grandmother wears a bright white headdress, and long drapes
of veil cover her dark dress – either she was still in mourning,
or there was not enough white cloth available in the freshly
cut-off eastern province of the German Empire. She might be
smiling, or attempting a smile that more resembles a smirk. My
great-grandfather has a large moustache and wears a dark suit
with a high white collar and a white tie. He's looking straight
at the camera with the sombre focus of a tribal chieftain, his
back erect and hands on his knees. Next to the bridal couple
are an old priest with strangely large hands, and my great-
grandfather's sister Theresa, a nun, wearing her habit with not
one but two crucifixes, one around her neck and one around
her hips. There are other couples and a few single guests,
mostly men wearing dark suits. One or two are in uniform but
without the insignia of the German Empire. The war to end all

wars, the Great War, had ended only the year before, and out of defeat and revolution the German Republic was born. But it seems the new army, the small *Reichswehr*, had not yet issued proper uniforms to their soldiers. Or the men in the picture had no better clothes to wear to a wedding than the uniforms of a recently deceased empire.

Cilly was born into a troubled place. Most of West Prussia and the province of Posen, territories annexed by Prussia in the eighteenth century and which linked East Prussia to Pomerania and Berlin, were ceded to the newly created Second Polish Republic in the Treaty of Versailles. East Prussia became an exclave, separated from mainland Germany. There was an air of suspicion and insecurity, of mistrust and paranoia which was particularly directed at the newly created country now surrounding East Prussia on almost all sides: Poland.

The *Seedienst Ostpreußen*, the East Prussian Sea Service, was established in 1920 to provide an independent transport service to East Prussia via the Baltic Sea. Overland transport to mainland Germany proved to be problematic, with train windows covered with curtains and some trains completely sealed for the duration of the trip through Polish territory. As a result of the demise of so many European empires in 1918, there was constant fighting around East Prussia: Estonia, Finland, Latvia and Lithuania declared independence from Russia and fought the Red Army to preserve their freedom, while fighting bloody civil wars against the Communists in their own countries. Throughout the existence of the Weimar Republic, there were constant border skirmishes with the new Polish Republic, which also had to fight off the Red Army in the Polish–Soviet war from 1919 to 1921, the remains of the shattered Russian armies surrendering to German troops on East Prussian territory.

Despite the times, Cilly found her parents' farm to be a peaceful place, an innocent haven of plenty. No one in the family had to go hungry, not even later during World War II. The farm was large – 47 hectares or 470,000 square metres – and self-sufficient. It took almost an hour to drive from the village to the large main farmhouse with a horse cart, past wheat fields and Lengainen lake, which was part of the farm's plot, as were dark woods and large expanses of grassland. It wasn't one of the biggest estates in East Prussia. There were farms with over 300 hectares, all owned by old Prussian nobility. The farm of my great-grandparents, however, was as large as a middle-class estate could grow in the sometimes medieval class structures of pastoral East Prussia.

My great-grandparents rarely left the farm. The only exception was for Mass. My great-grandfather Johannes was a pious man, and took his family to church every Sunday in the family carriage or a large sleigh, depending on the weather, proudly drawn by two horses that were not employed for any other work. This was the only occasion for the family to mingle with other villagers and farmers. My great-uncle Otto, who was groomed to take over the farm, usually went to the village pub after Mass to play cards and drink, while Johannes and Ottilie packed up the other children and drove home.

Despite being from East Prussia, land of schnapps and beer and hearty food, Johannes was a teetotaller and his favourite pastime was singing hymns with his children while they were working in the fields or at home after supper. His sister, the nun, had her own room at the farmhouse for when she was visiting, a small altar next to her bed bearing a crucifix, votive pictures of saints and the Virgin Mary. Hospitality played a huge part in the everyday life of the family. Every visitor, rare as they were, was plied with food and drink whatever the time of day. Cake and coffee in the afternoon, hearty meals with fatty soups, pork cutlets, chicken, steaming potatoes smothered in dark gravy or topped with butter and sprinkled with parsley for dinner, all accompanied by wine, beer and schnapps from the well-stocked drinks cabinet of my great-grandfather, only kept to make guests happy. After dinner, men smoked cigars overlooking the rolling hills, lakes and forests that slowly darkened in the setting sun. But it was not all agricultural romanticism: my great-grandfather fought long legal battles against the Prussian state for keeping all of his children out of school during harvest season. They were cheap labour, after all.

My first stop in Olsztyn is at the Polish–German Youth Centre, a beige building in the shadow of the castle, which also rents out rooms and where I'll stay for the next two weeks. It feels more like a hotel than a youth centre, even though a few German kids are lounging around in the downstairs restaurant. My room is terribly hot but, despite the lack of air conditioning, I like it. There's a desk, a large window opening out to a small terrace, and it looks right over a leafy park and the River Łyna. After unpacking, I walk around town.

Olsztyn has changed a lot since Cilly's time working in the fields nearby: the Stare Miasto, or Old Town, beneath the looming red-brick castle has been rebuilt, but outside the former city walls and away from the tourists who congregate here, Olsztyn is a working town with jobs mostly provided by the former state-owned tyre factory and the many administrative offices of the local government. It is home to 200,000 people and the University of Warmia and Masuria. Some of the old city walls remain and clearly mark the boundaries of the Old Town which sits on a hilltop with cobblestone lanes and squares, and alfresco terraces and beer gardens. There's a small amphitheatre right next to the hotel, with free open-air concerts and folkloric shows.

I have a beer and a burger at a steakhouse on a square in front of the old town hall, which is adorned with waist-high plastic sculptures, replicas of early medieval stone statues found all around Olsztyn. Called *Baba Pruska*, the statues depict a woman or a warrior with a drinking horn. No one's really sure about the purpose of these statues, though one theory says they were used to honour warriors who died far from home. Other explanations link the figures to legends of people turned to stone by witchcraft. I guess any female idol is a good omen for my trip, so I toast the Baba and order another beer.

Looking at the houses surrounding the square, I try to imagine what it was like in 1945, when smoke was rising from the wooden houses under the castle, in the snow. Though there was no battle for Allenstein, and the first few days of Russian occupation were quiet, some days later a fire started in the Old Town. Whether Red Army soldiers accidentally set fire to a house while looting it, or German owners deliberately burned their homes to stop their possessions falling into Russian hands, no one knows. But one thing is for sure: on 25 January, Allenstein burned to the ground.

Vassily Grossman, war correspondent with the Red Army, wrote after entering East Prussia in 1945:

> Millions of our men have now seen the rich farms in East Prussia, the highly organised agriculture, the concrete sheds for livestock, spacious rooms, carpets, wardrobes full of clothes. Millions of our soldiers [...] have seen the two-storey suburban houses with electricity, gas, bathrooms and beautifully tended gardens [...] And thousands of soldiers repeat these angry questions when they look around them in Germany: 'But why did they come to us? What did they want?'

~

The soldiers and their horses are tired. They trudge along the road leading from Allenstein, ochre bags and chipped rifles banging against the backs of the riders, who are squinting through half-closed eyes at the snow and the road beyond. They have come a long way since they started fighting the German invaders in 1941; initially, most of them were drafted into the new regiments and divisions that were thrown straight into the maw of the Battle of Stalingrad in 1942, half without rifles, and the ones with rifles with only one clip of ammunition. But those who survived have acquired sufficient rifles, they've been well fed and equipped with the best weapons the Russian factories in the Urals and the lend-lease transports from the UK and US could provide. With their new American trucks and *Katjuscha* rocket launchers, they formed the spearhead of the first-ever Soviet offensive against German territory. Now, after fighting the Germans for four years and endless miles, they have finally entered East Prussia. They captured Allenstein without any fighting, but now there are dark clouds of smoke rising from the town as they march away from it.

Many Soviet soldiers had been fighting for three years or more, and the Red Army did not offer any home leave. Men stayed with their units until they were wounded, or killed, or until the war was won. They had seen what the German invaders had done to their towns and villages, had seen the scorched earth of Ukraine and Belorussia. They were pushed forwards by relentless propaganda, their own commissars and political NKVD troops, the predecessor of the KGB. They entered a country with neat and colourful villages, well-maintained country lanes, and full larders and barns, and most of them must have asked themselves, like Grossman, why the Germans had brought war to Russia in the first place.

The column of 245 cavalrymen of the 3rd Guards Cavalry Corps of the Red Army riding from Allenstein are given the task of clearing the surrounding villages of stray German troops, eliminating any potential threat to the rearguard of the Soviet offensive. So far, all troops had reached their target areas without problem – most German troops and many civilians seemed to have fled. Their submachine guns and carbines clank against the cooking gear slung over their backs, their sabres rattle against their saddles.

~

You won't find any Germans here,' Rafael snorts. 'They have all left. Don't you know that all Poles living here now came from the East themselves?'

Rafael is an angry young Pole with short blond hair, two black eyes and impressive biceps. We've struck up conversation at a small bar overlooking the castle and my hotel. First we talk about beer and Ireland and then, after the second or third bottle of the strong dark local beer called Warmiak, we walk outside for a smoke. Rafael is an angry, but otherwise pleasant, man. I never find out what he is angry about. He introduces me to two girls who are sitting on a bench next to the entrance, but after he starts puffing on a stinky hand-rolled cigarette and I blow out the first puff of smoke from my pipe, they go back inside.

'So you're looking for traces of your grandmother?' he asks, vaguely gesturing with his cigarette at the castle. 'I don't think anyone here is going to talk to you. Most Poles around here were born someplace else. Haven't you heard of the flight and expulsion of the Poles?'

I had, just a few hours before. In the castle museum I had walked through a small exhibition dedicated to the so-called 'repatriation' of Poles, from the eastern areas of Poland annexed by the Soviet Union after 1945 to the former German areas of East Prussia, Pomerania and Silesia. The Poles who came to the Olsztyn area were mostly from Ukraine or Lithuania, and a few glass display cabinets in a reconstructed living room from Vilnius showed pictures, letters and other mementos of the former homeland, exactly like similar museums in Germany dedicated to the memory of East Prussia.

'And there's another thing: no one wants to talk about stories of yesteryear anyway. It's all about the future in Poland now.' Rafael flips his cigarette butt into the dark, sending sparks flying, empties his bottle and pushes himself up.

'Anyhow, you'll find me here most nights. You can buy me a beer and tell me how your search goes. Goodnight!'

The next morning, I find noisy kids clambering around Nicolaus Copernicus' shoulders and into his lap, smearing his robe with ice cream. His face is turned skywards and carries an expression of aloofness. Children have been smearing him with ice cream for the last 30 years after all, so he doesn't really care. He's even oblivious to my hangover, and I turn my back to the statue and shuffle up the lane to the main square to find breakfast.

At the terrace of a restaurant I wolf down a cheese omelette, wash it down with coffee and start to feel a bit better. I stayed at the bar, named Pozytywka, after Rafael had gone. I just wanted one last glass for the road, but then a concert started. The band was an old-school Klezmer orchestra with a fiddle, double bass and tuba, who premiered their latest music video to family and friends. The video was about a village wedding gone wrong, the beautiful bride leaving her old and wrinkled groom to run away with the female singer of the band, who was dressed as a man. In the bar they served lard bread and cheese-covered pastries and vodka, and men were dressed in three-piece suits and women wore skirts and bodices and everyone was drinking and singing along. At some point in the evening, all the lard bread, draught beer and vodka was gone, and the fridge was being emptied of its last few beer bottles. Sweat was dripping from the ceiling, everyone was dancing and I felt intensely happy and safe, until the vodka started going to my head and I chose to retire, leaving the singing and fiddling to guide me down the hill to my hotel. As I fell asleep I wondered what music would have been playing at local festivals in Lengainen or in the village pub, and if Cilly ever went along.

There's a black-and-white picture of my grandmother with a friend or admirer sitting in the grass in front of the farm building; she is wearing a striped dress and tights, and shoes with bows, her head slightly tilted to the left, away from him; her arms are crossed in her lap and they don't touch. He's wearing a black or blue sailor's uniform with a wide and jaunty cap embroidered with the German eagle and a swastika, a tall collar with white stripes and black boots. Cilly is looking upwards into the camera with what might be a thin smile; his gaze is serious despite their relaxed pose, and he looks at something next to Cilly's feet. She was 21 when she was taken, so she must have had boyfriends, lovers, but were they all from Lengainen? Or did she venture further out, to parties and concerts in Allenstein, perhaps? Her whole adolescence and teenage years were spent in East Prussia, but even after the work on the farm there must have been outings with friends, maybe late-night drinking near a lake, with a fire and the summer sun setting

4 Cilly and unknown friend, 1930s

behind the woods. Or am I projecting memories of my own adolescence onto hers?

I decide to find a lake myself, to escape the heat and the hangover, and to think. According to the brochure from the tourist office, there are 11 lakes within the city boundaries, so it shouldn't be too hard to find one. From the Old Town I walk through the Łyna river park, emerge between two rows of crumbling houses from the 1950s, and have to cross a two-lane roundabout before I reach the first lake, which is fenced in and has no grassland or benches. Walking and sweating along another small road, I finally discover another lake in a park right next to a concrete high-rise estate. Here, I find Polish girls sitting separately on park benches, each with a bench of her own, doing nothing except looking at the screens of their mobile phones from time to time. It's unnerving. They're not even sunbathing. Again, I wonder at how alien foreign countries can be, even ones that are not even 600 kilometres away from home, an insignificant distance in this interconnected world of ours. After a moment, I decide to finally visit Lengainen the next day. Maybe the past can bring me closer to the Poland of today.

Lengainen is an abstract image for me. I know what the farm looked like from the drawing my father made and some pictures in one of the photo albums Cilly left, rural scenes with almost stereotypical rural characters: my muscular, blond great-uncle Otto loading hay onto a cart, my grandmother milking a cow in a field, an older farmhand standing next to a strong dark horse towering over him. I don't think that the village of Lengainen, or Łęgajny today, where Cilly was born, itself ever played a huge role in her stories. It was all about the farm and the fields for her – it was my father who first told me the name of the village. I knew that it was part of the district of Allenstein. In 1939, 751 people lived here. There was a small chapel and a school, and a lake. In a photo album in my father's desk, there is a picture of Cilly with two or three siblings and an older female relative, wearing a bathing suit and posing for the camera on a slope that must have led down to that lake – 'At Lengainen lake', it says on the back of the picture.

I manage to get hold of a rental car, which involves walking past a six-lane arterial road to the local Holiday Inn while swearing at the July heat and the cars whooshing past. After acquiring my white Ford, I take the road to Lengainen. After a 15-minute drive past villages, small lakes and plastic noise protection walls I almost overlook the exit to Łęgajny. I drive past a statue of the Virgin Mary in the main street through the village, itself quite unspectacular. There are some newly built houses, a few sandstone buildings, one old sandstone chapel that looks like it dates from the nineteenth century, and a newer church behind it. It is a place halfway between an agricultural village and a suburb. I leave the car for a few minutes and take some photos, but as there is absolutely nothing hinting at buildings older than the chapel, I drive on. I don't know where the farm of my grandmother was located, so I set out to find the lake. Driving past the village sign only a few minutes after leaving the church, I encounter a seemingly distressed middle-aged woman in shorts and a black T-shirt, straying from one side of the road to the other. The car in front of me gives her a wide berth and drives on, but I decide to stop. After a quick exchange through the car window we establish that we have no common language, but that does not prevent her from walking around the car, opening the passenger door and clambering in. It is only then that I smell the booze. She keeps mentioning Olsztyn over and over again, so I explain with hands and feet that I can only drop her off at the village entrance, right next to the Virgin Mary. Whatever she is looking for, maybe the holy lady can help. After dropping off the drunken woman, I drive around country lanes and past business parks and the old, crumpling Lengainen station for another 20 minutes or so. I feel strangely intimidated, as if the episode with the woman is a sign that nothing will come of my stay here, or confirms what Rafael prophesied – no one would or could talk to me about the Germans who once lived here. But then I start thinking about how well Cilly must have known this area, and that she might have taken the train from the same crumbling station building where I parked earlier. A few minutes later, I feel elated when I spot the lake after driving through a small housing estate, a little bowl of water framed by woods, lawns and a few lonely telephone poles. I can't get down to the water's edge, but at least I get to walk around for a few minutes, breathing in the fresh air which smells of grass and washing powder, and listening to the chirping of the crickets in the tall grass.

In 1937, my great-grandfather Johannes died of stomach cancer in his bed surrounded by his family, after a long period of suffering. Cilly always told us that the family's large black dog lay at the foot of the bed and at the very moment of my great-grandfather's death let out a long, deep, sad howl that made everyone in the room shudder. The demise of the head of the household did not mean that the family business suffered. The eldest brothers took over. Otto Nerowski was a *bon vivant* with both a talent for numbers and a liking for women and drink. The pictures I have of him show a tall handsome man, either in a white working shirt with his chest showing or in suits, wearing his hair in the style of a Weimar Berlin dandy with his temples shaved and a slick blowdried hairdo on top. He was the one who connected Cilly with Solingen, my hometown. During the war, Otto travelled all over Germany to find customers for the farm's products – and one of these was a family named Maus, living in the small town of Solingen in the west of Germany, a connection that Cilly would one day benefit from.

Otto used to go to the village pub regularly to play cards and get drunk. To enable him to hold his drink against the other men, he used a trick: he always brought a thermos filled with coffee to the evenings at the pub. Before he left the house,

5   Barabasch family, ca. 1932 (Front row left to right: Lucie, Monika, Ottilie, Bruno, Cilly; back row left to right: Franz, Otti, Otto)

he made Cilly fry some bacon and pour the fat into the coffee, so he had a proper *Grundlage* or foundation for the local schnapps and beers.

My great-uncles, like my great-grandmother, disapproved of the Nazi regime. Otto preferred to do business with Jews because of their honesty and thoroughness, and his brother Franz, who worked as a teacher and a clerk for the Polish-owned Slavic Bank in Allenstein and later in Berlin, was one of the founding members of the local branch of the Union of Poles in Germany in 1935. He was the first family member to fall to the Nazis. Franz was drafted into the Wehrmacht in 1937 and served in the invasion of Poland in 1939 – but his sympathies always lay with the Poles. This was the reason why he started working for the Polish resistance after the fall of Poland, supplying information about the Wehrmacht to them under the code name 'Późny'. He was arrested on home leave in 1940 and spent two years in prisons in Berlin and Brandenburg, before he was guillotined for treason on 21 August 1942. He was 32 years old.

After his brother's death, Otto escaped the waves of forced drafting that swept through Germany after 1943, and the appalling losses on the Eastern Front. Growing food for the fatherland was deemed important enough to earn him exemption and he stayed at home until he was finally drafted into the

6 Death sentence of Franz Nerowski, 1942

Wehrmacht in 1944. He went missing in action, somewhere in the East. By then, Cilly's older sisters had married and left the farm, so in the end it was only herself, her mother and the youngest siblings Monika and Bruno working on the farm, together with two French POWs as forced labour. It is easy to see that while the family of my grandmother was harvesting the last crop of their secure island in the autumn light of 1944, darkness was already gathering around them. There was a former nursing home in Allenstein serving as a makeshift prison where the captured Gypsies of this part of East Prussia were slowly starving to death, awaiting transportation to a concentration camp. After getting rid of one brother, the local authorities were already eagerly eyeing and circling the estate, waiting for Otto to be drafted into the Wehrmacht. The hungry skies over Germany, and their machine-gun and anti-aircraft fire, were waiting to devour my great-uncle Bruno on his first flight. And somewhere in Russia, a cattle wagon was being prepared for Cilly.

~

'Cilly, are you coming? Mother is waiting for you with the coffee.'

She gazes out over the small lake, frozen and still, takes a final pull from her cigarette, throws the butt down towards the shore, and then looks up towards the fence on the hill where her little sister Monika is standing.

'I'm coming.'

~

I have to take her cigarette away here. It made a nice picture at first, her smoking, lost in thought, looking out over the frozen lake. But she did not smoke at the time – she only picked up the habit in Russia later on, my father told me. So I'll keep her lungs clean for the moment. There's enough smoke in the air already in January 1945. Her hair is a mess of brown-black curls again, and I imagine her wearing another thick scarf in the February cold, this one blue, together with a dark coat and thick brown boots. That's how I often think of her, waiting in winter, for me and the Soviet secret service to arrive.

~

Cilly stomps up the small hill and, grabbing her sister, puts her in a headlock.

'Ah Cilly, my hair! Leave it!'

Monika is always concerned about her looks, already, at 14. Cilly laughs and shoves her up the hill.

'Let's run – the winner gets the biggest piece of cake!'

They both laugh and sprint up the hill, throwing up snow behind them like hares turning corners running away from wolves. At the farmhouse they stop, and walk through the door after pausing to stomp their boots free of snow. Inside, their mother has laid the table in the kitchen, with the good porcelain. It smells of *Ersatzkaffee*, malt coffee substitute, and the cake that their mother has made that morning. They sit down and Ottilie says the Lord's Prayer. It's not yet four in the afternoon but already growing dark. They eat in silence for a while, as if the familiar ritual of afternoon coffee allows them some insight into the events of the last few days. Cilly thinks she smells burning wood coming from outside.

The men really looked like the Mongols that Herr Goebbels was always ranting about on the radio when they rode up towards the farm. Six shaggy horses on which sat six small, broad men, their faces covered with dust and grime, their eyes squinting as they scanned the farmhouse and the barn. Only after two of them had climbed down from their saddles and, having searched both the farmhouse and the outbuildings, waved to the others did they relax, the muzzles of their stocky submachine guns and rifles coming to point at the ground. All were wearing stained light-brown uniform coats; some had round steel helmets in the same colours, and others padded fur hats that covered their ears. Cilly, Monika and their mother stood pressed together in front of the farmhouse, the elderly French POW farmhand Maurice behind them. After the men stepped closer they suddenly stopped – confused by the bread and steaming cups of coffee that Monika and Cilly were offering on trays. For a moment they seemed reluctant, but then the man in the first row, an elderly soldier with grey hair, laughed out loud and grabbed a cup. Cilly relaxed as the other men gathered around her and took pieces of bread and the remaining mugs. But when she looked around, she saw two of the soldiers leading Monika towards the barn, while a third pushed Maurice against the wall of the farmhouse, all of the soldiers still laughing. The bearded man drained his coffee, threw the mug behind him as Ottilie gasped and then, gently, took the empty tray from Cilly's hands, set it down and grabbed her elbow, steering her towards the barn as well.

∼

I will stop here. I won't write about my grandmother being raped. It happened, and it happened to women often during the Red Army invasion. Berlin women had a saying, referring to both the repeated rapes after the Battle of Berlin and the Allied bombing: 'Better a Russian on the belly than an American on the head.' But when the Red Army reached Berlin, they had already been on German soil for three months. East Prussia was the first German territory they entered, and here the violence towards women was extreme. As described in his eyewitness account of the East Prussia invasion, 'To Be Preserved for Ever', Red Army officer Lev Kopelev found a woman lying in her own bed in a sea of blood – after a group of Red Army soldiers had raped her, they stabbed her repeatedly with cheap plastic knives. I cannot attempt to replicate in fiction the experiences of Red Army soldiers in East Prussia in 1945, or the experiences of the German women. I can just point out that it happened. Let's get back to that coffee in the kitchen a couple days later. I'm on safer ground there. At least I know what's coming.

~

Cilly is doing the washing up, her mother is cleaning the table and Monika looks out of the kitchen window, from where you can see the road leading up to the farm.

'Cilly! Someone's driving up the road!'

The men come to the farm on 10 February 1945, in the early afternoon. Four men in an open jeep, wearing grey winter coats with red patches on their collars and the red star of the Soviet Union on their sleeves. Two have stocky Russian submachine guns with round magazines over their laps, one is driving, and the last, wearing the largest fur hat of all, is holding a clipboard, apparently an officer. Cilly dries her hands on her apron and joins their mother at the door. The two men with the machine guns jump from the jeep and scan the buildings, while the man with the clipboard walks straight towards them, the motor of the car idling.

'Are you Ottilie Barabasch?' the man asks in German.

'Yes?' Cilly's mother answers.

'You are hereby ordered to appear tomorrow at the main Lengainen collection point in front of the chapel. You will be taken to work in Mohrungen for a few days.'

He rips a slip of paper from his clipboard and pushes it into my great-grandmother's hands.

'What work?' Cilly bursts out, regretting it as the officer angrily stares at her.

'What do you care? Farm work, from what I know.'

She doesn't think about it too long.

'But why take my mother? She's an old woman and would not be of any use to you. Can you not take me instead?'

The officer looks her up and down. His eyes are dark brown. He shrugs and takes the slip of paper back from Ottilie.

'Your name?'

'Cäcilie Barabasch.'

His pen scratches across the paper on his clipboard, and he hands Cilly another slip of paper.

'You meet tomorrow, nine in the morning, at the church in the village.' He turns and walks back towards the jeep, jumps in and drives away with the other men, who all stare straight ahead. They have more names on their list.

'What was that about?' Ottilie asks.

~

In 1943, academic Ivan Maisky, the Soviet ambassador to the UK and deputy in the People's Commissariat of Foreign Affairs, was ordered to form a task force on the issue of postwar reparations. Maisky's report, finally issued in August 1944, proposed the employment of German civilian labour in the USSR as part of war reparations. At the Yalta Conference in 1945, Stalin made it clear to the western Allies that he intended to employ German civilian labour, and neither Winston Churchill nor Theodore Roosevelt raised any objections.

After Soviet troops entered German territory, the Soviet State Committee for the Defence of Germany, a newly founded authority to administer occupied German areas, issued a decree. Field troops of the NKVD, the Soviet secret service, were to mobilise all German men between the ages of 17 and 50 suitable for physical work and capable of bearing arms. Germans whose service in the Wehrmacht or *Volkssturm*, the national militia, was considered proven were to be sent to a prison camp. The remaining mobilised Germans were instructed to form labour battalions to be used as free workers in the USSR.

By 20 February 1945, 18 days after my grandmother was taken, 28,105 people, mostly women, had been taken in the operational areas to which the decree applied – mainly Upper Silesia and East Prussia. There were no men left for the NKVD to fulfil their quotas, so they brought the women instead.

~

Cilly packs for a few days. A long warm winter coat and a leather rucksack which she fills with two extra pairs of underwear, two jumpers and food: some gammon and cheese from the secret chamber in the barn that the Russians had not found. She's wearing a brown woollen scarf around her head and thick gloves. At the door, Ottilie and Monika hug her. Monika is sobbing.

'Don't cry. I'll be back soon. It's only for a few days anyway.'

Ottilie says nothing, just holds her daughter at arm's length and looks at her, before hugging her hard. This is the last time they will ever see each other, but they don't know this.

'We could have taken you in the sledge, had the bloody Russians left us the horses!'

'Never mind Mama, walking is fine. It won't snow for a while.'

Cilly sets off, past the empty barn and down the driveway, past the deserted fields and the frozen lake. She's wearing her sturdiest and warmest boots, the ones reserved for excursions to the forest in winter. There's no sound in the air, no thudding of faraway artillery or the drone of aeroplanes. It's almost as if the war has wandered off. After an hour she's in Lengainen, where a small group of women and girls are already waiting at the chapel, two women from Lengainen and two more from surrounding villages.

'Cilly, you too?' Erika Braun, the blonde, buxom daughter of the publican, asks.

'They wanted to take my mother, so I came in her place.'

'What do they want us to do? Did you also get a stupid slip of paper? I don't understand a word.'

'It's just a transfer order. We are supposed to report to the *Kommandantura*, the local Russian command post in Mohrungen.'

'And they believe we would go there freely? Across country when they are still fighting?'

'I'm not sure what they expect us to do…'

Cilly is cut off by the rumble of a truck coming down the main road from Allenstein. It's a dirty grey monster covered in a shredded tarpaulin. Two guards in brown winter coats and with submachine guns jump down from the platform as the truck skids to a halt on the snow- and mud-covered road.

'*Dawai! Dawai! Bistra!*' they shout and point their guns towards the truck. Cilly and the others clamber aboard and join a few other women who are already sitting on the floor clinging to one another. Cilly turns to Erika as the last women from Lengainen climb up.

'I guess that answers your question, doesn't it?'

3 DARK NIGHT

Oh aye,
We know violence;
It carefully nurtured us.
Insisted our mothers give birth to us
Prostrate and in stirrups.

Abby Oliveira, 'American Candy'

My grandmother was 'mobilised' on 10 February 1945. The
NKVD units informed the people of Lengainen that everyone
between the ages of 17 and 50 should report to the nearest official gathering point for 'a few days of light farm work'. People
were advised to bring clothing for 15 days. Often these orders
were followed without the need for the NKVD to assign guards
– refusal to obey these offers would only mean retaliation by
the Russians. My grandmother was first taken to Mohrungen,
60 kilometres away. I don't know if the Red Army provided
transport for the prisoners, or if they had to cover the distance
on foot. But for the moment, I decide to give them a ride in a
truck.

~

The truck rumbles on across the frozen streets and lanes of
East Prussia, sometimes overtaking marching soldiers, sometimes stuck in traffic jams behind tanks belching out black
smoke, elderly Red Army soldiers in horse-drawn carts and the
occasional small group of downtrodden East Prussian civilians. The truck stops from time to time and more people are

forced to climb inside. The NKVD soldiers make them sit in a row, each prisoner sat inside the opened legs of the one behind him, like a twisted version of a children's game. The guards laugh when arranging the prisoners. Cilly, Erika and the other women try to stay together in a group. After another hour of shaking and rumbling, the truck stops and the tailboard is opened. '*Dawai!* All out!'

'Where are we?'

Erika points to a street sign.

'Mohrungen.'

The captives are marched from the truck through the middle of the village, towards a longish brown building with a red roof and three storeys: the local school. There are no children any more.

~

I'm late and I'm lost. I'm driving through seemingly endless Polish forests on a small road. There are no turnings or exits, just the one road unspooling ahead. A while ago, I took the wrong turning at an Olsztyn roundabout and now I am here. According to my map, there should be a turning that will lead me to Stawiguda and Frau Moritz, but my confidence is shot. I'm struggling to believe there is anything up ahead other than further shadowy forest.

I made contact with the local society of the German minority two days ago. Their office is in a newly renovated townhouse from the nineteenth century, and when I showed up I was welcomed by the small, energetic Frau Barczewski. This stocky, resolute lady with long white hair had the friendly East Prussian accent I had previously only heard from Cilly and her siblings: rolling the Rs and sharply emphasising the vowels, closer to a Yiddish accent than anything else. Frau Barczewski listened to my story for a few minutes and then, stopping me

mid-sentence with a raised finger, picked up the phone and di-
alled a number. 'Gertrud? I've got a young man here, a writer,
who wants to talk to you about your time in Russia. Three
o'clock today? Yes, that's fine. I'll send him over.' In this way
my first meeting with a contemporary witness who had been
in the same camp as my grandmother was arranged.

Finally, I come to the village where Gertrud Moritz lives,
after driving past a small lake, which I mentally bookmark for
a dip later on. It is still as hot and muggy as hell as I arrive at
the cobblestoned main road in Stawiguda, or Stabigotten as it
was called during German times. 'The first road behind the
church, and if you're lost just ask someone – Frau Moritz is
known all over the place,' Frau Barczewski had said. But my
recent attempts to make conversation with non-English-
speaking Poles have not been encouraging, which means I try
to find Frau Moritz's home on my own, adding another five
minutes' delay. When I finally find the house in a side street, I
feel relieved.

I walk through the open door into a cramped but tidy
kitchen, and a small elderly lady, in a blue skirt and a red
jumper with wild red hair and glasses, shuffles in from an an-
teroom.

'That is not very German, your tardiness! But come in,
come in.'

Frau Moritz walks with a stoop, and age must have shrunk
her a bit as she hardly comes up to my chest, but it does not
seem to have otherwise slowed her down. She has set the table
in her living room with coffee and marble cake and Streusel
slices, and I'm reminded of Cilly, of the same tidy way she used
to set her table with the same choice of cakes. Also present is
Renate, a neighbour, who is a few years younger and some
stones heavier than Frau Moritz. After we sit down I give them
my spiel about being a writer who is searching for traces of my
grandmother, and again I'm stopped mid-sentence by a raised
hand.

'First the coffee and the cake, young man, then the old stories.'

Gertrud Moritz was 20 in 1945 and working as the local postwoman when she was taken, along with other girls from the area. Her younger sister, 15 years old at the time, was left behind, and Gertrud hoped that her sister would stay with her mother in their village. 'I was told to pack for two days of work, and that we would be taken to Hohenstein for farm work. In the end, they only moved us to a village nearby, Sensutten, where we had to sleep in a saw mill amidst the sawdust.' From here, like my grandmother, she was taken to Mohrungen.

'And from Mohrungen we were brought to Insterburg, and from there on straight to paradise, ha!'

She lives with her daughter and grandson now, who also joins us for a short while and addresses her as *Oma*, granny. The living room is tidy, and there's a shelf with trinkets, pictures and a souvenir replica of Cologne Cathedral.

'Young man, you actually don't need to write anything down. You can just copy from me!' Frau Moritz laughs. She shuffles to her bedroom and returns with a manila folder. It seems she's a media pro and I am not the first to come asking. She has the postcards she sent from Russia to her family in West Germany via the Red Cross, copies of her file and even 14 loose pages filled with tidy handwriting – her own story, written down in 2001. 'When my memory and my handwriting still served me well, haha.'

The meeting with Frau Moritz is my first interview with a contemporary witness, and I am a bit intimidated. But after a while I begin to feel more comfortable asking questions – and get a first glimpse of what it must have been like for Cilly, thanks to the lovely granny in front of me. I'm very thankful for meeting her.

'They came on the 15 February 1945, around noon. The soldiers told me to pack my things for two days, but then they kept us, and after passing through Hohenstein we were transferred to the prison in Insterburg. After a few days there they called out our names, put us in groups of 30–40 and packed us into livestock wagons. The train left the station and I don't know if it was bombs or artillery, but at one point there were explosions nearby and the train rolled back a few kilometres.'

There was still heavy fighting between the Red Army and Wehrmacht – the siege of nearby Königsberg lasted until April 1945.

'But after that, slowly, slowly, the train picked up speed and we were on our way. For three weeks we travelled eastwards, with them throwing in food – dry rusks and water – once a day. We finally arrived in a place called Nizhny Tagil.'

I show her a picture of my grandmother and some of the information about the camp I have received from the Red Cross, and ask if she met a Frau Barabasch from Lengainen there.

'Unfortunately I don't think I met her – the camp was huge! There were even German prisoners of war who had fought in the Battle of Stalingrad, thousands of people. How did your grandmother end up there?'

And then a strange thing happens. Frau Moritz keeps asking me questions about my grandmother, about her family, the camps she was in, and her work in Russia. And for a short moment, while I try to answer her questions to the best of my ability, it is as if I have become a stand-in for Cilly, as if she is speaking through me, answering questions that she is asked but can no longer answer.

'We worked on roads, in a quarry and whatnot. After half a year I was transferred to a farm camp in Aksarka near the Ob River in northern Russia. I stayed there until 1947, when I caught typhus and was transferred back to Germany. I would not have made it much longer – at the end my weight was only 40 kilos.'

Frau Moritz decided to go back to Allenstein and Stabigotten – a decision not shared by many women in her group. She first had to spend a couple of days in Berlin at the Polish Embassy and at another transfer camp, but then she was put on a train heading to East Prussia, or what she perceived as East Prussia. It had already become Warmia-Masuria.

'You see, my mother was still there, and I thought my sister Teresa would be as well, and I never would have left them if I could have helped it. My sister was taken a few days after me and died in the camps – but I did not find out until I returned. So first they put me in a quarantine camp on the island of Rügen, and from there I travelled to Berlin to get my papers. And once on the train, when we crossed the Oder, they told us to stop speaking German as we were Poles now. But I made it back to Stabigotten and here I am still.'

Gertrud Moritz never left her village after she returned. In 1961, she married a young German man from the area, Bernhard Moritz, with whom she had two children. And even though she sometimes had the urge to return to Russia to see what had become of the area around her old camp, she never did. 'I'm glad that I stayed here. Russia taught me what longing for home means. And I now know what it means to be here, at home.'

~

In the school, the women are brought to an empty classroom, where they have to sleep on the bare floor, without mattresses or blankets. The door is locked, and escaping via the third-floor windows is impossible. In the deserted classroom the desks are like a terrified herd, driven one upon another in a corner of the room, scattered about with the inkstands torn loose. On the wall is the music and first stanza of the national anthem, 'The Song of the Germans' by Hoffmann von Fallersleben. Next to this, there's a map of the *Großdeutsches*

Reich, the greater German Reich, with all territories occupied by the Wehrmacht – long since made obsolete by American, British and Russian soldiers and tanks. The blackboard is lying face down on the teacher's desk, and Cilly sits down against it. Here is another proof of the hubris of the Nazis, she thinks, crying women held capture by victorious Red Army troops in a classroom that is no longer needed.

Some of the women only have the clothes they were wearing when they were captured. Cilly is thankful for the food she packed. They aren't allowed to wash, and can only visit the toilet once a day under the supervision of the guards. They are freezing. As the classroom isn't heated, the meagre February sun behind the frozen windows is their only source of warmth. No food is handed out by the guards, and Cilly sometimes shares a few morsels from her rations with the others, but she is reluctant to give everything out. How long will the Russians leave them here, without food?

'What do they want with us?' one of the women asks.

'They told me I would only need to help out on a farm for a few days,' Erika says. 'Then I could go home.'

'Girl, I think we're in this for much longer than a couple of days…'

In the evening they hear male and female voices from a room across the corridor, Red Army soldiers singing Russian songs. The strange, foreign melodies drift into the classroom through the closed door. The other women don't understand the words, but Cilly likes to listen to the songs, which sound much sadder than German marching songs, hinting at longing and love. Russian singer Sidor Belarsky recorded exemplary lyrics in his famous Soviet wartime song 'Dark Night':

Still I believe,
Trusting you, dear spouse of mine.
In these dark nights, only this faith,
Kept me safe from a bullet.

After two days on the classroom floor, they are taken from the school under the watch of ten armed guards and marched through the streets. Mohrungen is a middle-sized town of 8,000 inhabitants, 50 kilometres north of Allenstein. Groups of prisoners from other parts of town join them and the procession grows. There are only women and girls, and Cilly watches two elderly women with dirty grey headscarves being taken right from the pavement, screaming and shouting, as the column marches past. Whenever there is a halt, everyone tries to scatter off to try to find bits of clothing or something to eat in one of the surrounding deserted houses, as much as the guards allow. Cilly walks with Erika to one small house next to the street, with one of the guards indicating that he has seen them and expects them to be back soon. Inside the hall and front room, there's chaos. The furniture, pictures and doors have been smashed with rifle butts; excrement is on the floor in every room. The back of the house does not look any better. When the Russians needed a room, they just threw everything inside out of the window. They find nothing to eat.

Soon there's another call of '*Dawai!*', and the column sets off. The buildings they walk past are in ruins, some still smouldering. As they reach the hospital, a large white building, there's a loud gasp and then a few cries from the front. As Cilly comes closer, she sees why: the male patients, wounded soldiers, have been thrown from the windows of the three-storey building. They are lying in the forecourt in their blue-and-white striped pyjamas, their limbs spread out in all directions, fingers and arms and bare feet rigid from rigor mortis pointing skywards and at the women. There is no glass on the ground, so the Russians must have taken the time to open the windows first.

Everywhere on the pavements and in the bushes are ransacked bags, rucksacks and briefcases, the contents strewn across the street. Without thinking, Cilly grabs a linen bag filled with colourful balls of wool. She is wondering why the fugitives have taken wool with them on their flight – there must have been more important items. Suddenly, loud cheering and shouting is heard from behind them. The women shriek and move closer to the bushes at the side of the road and away from the street. A group of men in civilian clothes is riding up and down the street in horse-drawn sledges, laughing and jeering and sipping from glass bottles, some of them wearing women's clothes, bits and pieces of German uniforms and briefcases and bags stacked on the cart, leaving a trail of paper streaming behind them as they dash past the women. They shout to each other in Polish, and Cilly thinks they must be either freed farmworkers or Poles celebrating the German defeat.

'Listen to those Poles. It's like the Thirty Years' War all over again, isn't it?' Erika whispers to Cilly.

'*Dawai!* Move!' the guards shout and the column starts moving off again. There are more trucks waiting for them and the other prisoners, their number now around 200.

If my grandmother was something like a Nazi Dorothy, then the evil Wizard of Oz also had his lair in East Prussia. After driving for an hour through shady woods and past lakes that glisten in the sun, I reach my destination, not far from the town of Kętrzyn. As I turn into a small driveway off a quiet forest road, I'm surprised to see a black armoured personnel carrier coming towards me, smiling tourists with sunglasses and straw hats sitting on the open top. As they drive past, I stop at a wooden hut where a security guard dressed in a black uniform sells me a ticket and directs me to a crowded car park. I spray myself with mosquito repellent – as Lonely Planet suggests – before getting out of the car and emerging into the baking summer heat. Behind the car park is a small hotel and restaurant – in a former bunker, as the sign out front tells me in four languages – and a few souvenir shops. There's also a wooden stand, half-hidden in camouflage netting, where you can have your picture taken in a German uniform, riding a Wehrmacht motorbike or aiming an MG-42 machine gun from behind sandbags. A beautiful young woman dressed in hot pants and a camouflage jacket that looks way too warm in the July sun is handing out flyers to passing visitors. The car park is full of picnicking families and children licking ice creams, and it all resembles an amusement park and not the former command centre of the German army in World War II.

The *Wolfsschanze*, or Wolf's Lair, was Adolf Hitler's first Eastern Front military headquarters. The complex, which was one of several *Führerhauptquartiere* (Führer Headquarters) located in various parts of occupied Europe, was built for Operation Barbarossa – the invasion of the Soviet Union – and constructed by Organisation Todt, the Nazi engineering group. Hitler first arrived at the headquarters in June 1941. In total, he spent more than 800 days at the Wolf's Lair until his final departure on 20 November 1944. On 25 January 1945, 14 days before my grandmother was taken to Russia, the complex was blown up and abandoned so it would not fall into the hands of the Red Army.

Although three security zones surrounded the central complex where the Führer bunker was located, the Wolf's Lair was also where Claus von Stauffenberg famously attempted to kill Hitler with a bomb on 20 July 1944. Today, the site and the visitor centre, administered by the Polish state, are operated by a private company and are one of the main tourist attractions in Warmia-Masuria. Visitors can stay in the former building of Hitler's personal security headquarters, where a hotel and restaurant have now opened, and there is even an airsoft shooting range in the former staff bunker of General Alfred Jodl, Chief of the Operations Staff of the Armed Forces High Command of the Wehrmacht. Stepping out from the parking area under the dark canopy of trees that have grown over the bunkers, the memorial to Stauffenberg is the first thing I encounter. Two small plaques mark the location of the wooden barracks where the assassination attempt took place. The German resistance had planned to kill Hitler during a meeting in his bunker, where the bomb blast would have had maximum effect, but due to the warm weather in July 1944, the meeting was moved to the barracks. Although the bomb went off, it could not deliver its hoped-for impact and Hitler survived.

I'm thankful for the shade of the trees surrounding the heaps of rubble that mark the locations of the bunkers. Some are better preserved than others, but everywhere the massive concrete walls impress me. The pieces and askew walls of 2-metre-thick, steel-reinforced concrete scattered around almost look natural. Maybe the ruins fit the view the Nazis had of themselves: look at what we can do, surely we are the master race. There are Polish families walking around, the men laughingly clambering into the bunkers where possible and over the rubble where not. German tourists in shorts and sandals are led around by tour guides in orderly groups, and overall there's no distinction between a visit to a medieval castle somewhere in France and the place where Hitler plotted world domination. I often think that Hitler is long gone, reduced to some kind of bogeyman used by neo-Nazis in East Germany and a horror authors use to evoke fear. Thousands of books have been written about the hubris of Hitler and his lackeys, and today the Wolf's Lair is not the place to reiterate all this. Instead, I'll try to elaborate what direct effects Hitler and his politics had on my grandmother and her family.

History never flows in a predictable way. It is always a result of seemingly random currents and incidents, the individual and overall significance of which can only be determined in hindsight. When I started gathering Cilly's stories and researching the history of East Prussia and of my family, I was convinced that this was a German story in the German tongue; about a neat and tidy German village invaded by the women-stealing Red Army, which it wasn't. Instead I found out that a large part of my family, especially my great-uncle Franz, identified themselves as – or at least sympathised with – Poles, or to be more specific, the Polish population of East Prussia. The area had always been one of distinct multiculturalism, a place where the old cultures of Poles, Germans, Lithuanians and even the old Masurian tribes had come together to trade, celebrate, blend. And this was also represented by place names. As painter and graphic artist Robert Budzinski states in his 1913 love declaration to East Prussia, 'The Discovery of East Prussia' (*Die Entdeckung Ostpreußens*):

> During my wanderings I continuously discovered places with not very known but quite illustrious names; so that I often thought I was roving about in a magical landscape. One day I took the train from Groß-Aschnaggern to Liegentrocken, Willpischken, Pusperschkallen and Katrinigkeiten, breakfasted in Karkeln, arrived in Pissanitzen, Bammeln, Babbeln, and had dinner in Pschintschikowsken while aiming to overnight in Karßamupchen.

It was only the landslide election victory of the Nazis in East Prussia in 1933 (56.5 per cent compared with the German average of 43.9 per cent), based on their promise to revise the pre-World War I borders, that brought an end to the open and sometimes cosmopolitan society of East Prussia. 'The lethargy of the constant thread of an island status was replaced by a sense of unity', as historian Andreas Kossert states in 'East Prussia – History of a Historical Landscape' (*Ostpreußen – Geschichte einer historischen Landschaft*, 2014). And that change was especially reflected in the place names introduced by the Nazis in 1938, when *Gauleiter* (Nazi district leader) Erich Koch announced the final renaming of all 'Slavic-sounding' place names to German ones: Wawrochen became *Deutschheide* (German heath), Suchorowitz became *Deutschwalde* (German forest), Achodden became *Neuvölklingen*

(New colony). Polish-language theological courses at Königsberg University were abandoned, and the churches in Allenstein were no longer allowed to hold services in Polish, a 600-year-old Protestant tradition.

Cilly spoke Polish before the Russians arrived, and her two half-brothers openly supported Polish self-determination in East Prussia. And yet, even though her brother Franz was executed as a Polish resistance fighter, Cilly's family lived through Nazi times and were neither shunned nor marked as outsiders.

Instead they lived and prospered as part of the German Reich, and while they might have privately disagreed with the regime that killed one of their sons, it still put food on their table and gave them French POWs as farmhands. And, as I mentioned, one of my other great-uncles was so enamoured of the Luftwaffe that he joined it, only to die on his first flight.

I didn't talk about Hitler and Nazi Germany a lot with Cilly. I do remember that we agreed that he was a bad man and that there were bad times during the war, but we never went deeper. But I can surely say that my grandmother, ten years old when the Nazis rose to power and coming of age in Hitler's Germany, never showed admiration for the Führer later in life. And then there's this: Cilly liked to tell the story of how Nazi officials came to the farm and tried to decorate my great-grandmother, Ottilie, with the Mother's Cross, the Iron Cross for women who gave the Führer and his Reich four children or more. It makes for a compelling scene: my matriarchal great-grandmother refuses the decoration and throws it at the feet of the lackey of the Reich (in my mind always wearing the long, shiny leather coat of the Gestapo and round spectacles, straight from *Indiana Jones*) who sneers and says something along the lines of 'You'll see us again, Frau Barabasch!' This was a story my grandmother told quite often, and my father keeps repeating it. For me, this is good ammunition against the possibility that any of my family might have collaborated with the Nazis, or even worse, become party members. And it's an indicator of how divided many similar families must have been across Germany and Europe, pledging allegiance to the Nazis and their enemies.

As I leave the forest of the Wolf's Lair to return to the car, I pass a booth selling, besides picture books of Wehrmacht tanks and German uniforms, booklets about the German resistance and Stauffenberg, and for a moment I am proud that one of my relatives was part of that resistance, even though it means he gave his life for it.

~

In February 1945, there are no trucks for Cilly and the others. They walk the 60 kilometres to Heilsberg, which is their next destination. Not that anyone tells the prisoners where they are going. They just plough on, through snow and mud. They pass the wrecks of carts and sleighs and wagons, as well as corpses, some pressed into the ground by tank tracks and the wheels of trucks, like hedgehogs run over by cars. This is what Cilly sees: the remnants of a desperate flight, smashed wardrobes and Sunday clothes strewn across muddy country lanes, the frozen faces of the dead.

Most inhabitants of East Prussia tried to flee as soon as the Russians fired the first shots. Many people had finalised their escape plans in October 1944, when the Red Army first invaded. These plans, however, had to be made in secret: despite the rapid advances of the Red Army, the German authorities and especially Gauleiter Erich Koch forbade leaving one's place of residence without a permit. The 2.5 million inhabitants of East Prussia were left in these areas until fighting overwhelmed them. When the German authorities finally gave people the order to leave, there was hardly any transport left.

Most people fled in groups made up of people from the same village or farm, collecting their belongings on carriages and carts, drawn by oxen and farm horses, with crude struc tures on the wagons made from old planks, carpets and canvas pieces to protect the pregnant women and small children inside. No one was able to take everything they owned, and what should one pack anyway? A cupboard? Books? Food? Many tried to take as much as possible, and the fleeing refugees must have looked like a biblical exodus. Some may have expected to return, especially when they remembered the brief Russian occupation of East Prussia in 1914, which was one of the reasons my great-grandmother decided to stay at the farm with Cilly and Monika – she was convinced that the Russians would leave again soon. But many must have felt that this was it: either the refugees would make it to the West with their lives and belongings, or they would perish. The Wehrmacht had treated the Soviet Union too badly, too many lives had been extinguished and too much land destroyed to allow any remorse on the side of the invading Red Army. And any remorse they may still have felt was finally extinguished by the propaganda from both Berlin and Moscow. Flee or perish – no other options existed in the minds of most refugees.

Slowly, the crude *treks* (named after the Boer migrations in South Africa in the nineteenth century) made their way west, trying to escape the advance of the Red Army by inching away via already crowded country lanes. They had few choices: either head west and try to reach the former Polish Corridor and Danzig across the Vistula; or head north and try to cross the frozen lagoon, the *Frisches Haff,* beyond which was a narrow sandy spit called the *Frische Nehrung.* The *Nehrung* would lead the refugees to Gotenhafen (Gdynia today) or Danzig – and to another escape route by sea. The last option, the most promising as long as trains were running, was to go north-east towards the capital of East Prussia, Königsberg, and its harbour Pillau, and escape across the Baltic Sea. In the event, whichever route they chose, most of the treks were overtaken by the Red Army which, in some cases, crashed through the refugee columns with their T-34 tanks. All the while, Cilly was moving in the other direction.

After a day of marching, the prisoners reach the Old Prussian settlement of Heilsberg, a once thriving town of 15,000 inhabitants that is now a smouldering heap of ruins. Like Allenstein, it was captured by the Red Army without a fight, but uncontrolled fires started a few days later and destroyed half of the town. The column is split up into smaller groups, and Cilly, Erika and a few others are confined to the basement of a private house. That night, Cilly is taken for interrogation for the first time. In the ruined living room, she is made to sit on a creaky chair opposite a Russian officer who relaxes on the sofa with a large pile of files next to him and a clipboard on his knee. Two soldiers holding carbines fitted with bayonets stand behind the sofa. The officer speaks German.

~

I possess a copy of my grandmother's NKVD file, obtained from the Red Cross, which still keeps records from all World War II POWs.

Cilly's file has four pages. Her details were first recorded on 12 February 1945, two days after she was taken. It gives the names of her parents and siblings, the location and size of the farm ('47 hectares, 12 cows, six horses'), the fact that she spoke Russian and Polish, her profession ('none – working on my parents' farm'), distinguishing features ('none') and has her signature at the bottom, a girlish squiggle translated into Cyrillic letters by one of her interrogators. Her address is Lengainen Estate, Lengainen, District Allenstein. Cäcilie Anna Barabasch was 21 when she was taken.

Cilly was officially a prisoner of war, not one of those political prisoners taken by the Soviets later, after their occupation of East Germany, so there was no trial for her, no extortion of

a confession as so often happened later. In the Soviet zone of occupation and later the German Democratic Republic

(GDR), there were countless basements across East Berlin, or former Nazi concentration camps like Sachsenhausen that were used as Soviet political prison camps until 1950, so-called 'silent camps' where all contact with the outside world was punishable by death. No, my grandmother was taken too early in the war, and so she did not become a political prisoner – not that it would have made a difference.

7 Cilly's Gupvi file, 1945

~

The Soviet officials just take her details and make her sign the statement, and then she is taken back to the basement, and the next prisoner brought up to provide the raw bones of her life for the NKVD archive in Moscow. Not knowing what will happen, the women hunker down and tremble whenever the key turns in the lock. With the morning light, two soldiers walk into the basement and search their belongings. Cutlery, needles, scissors, candles, matches are all taken. Strangely, the soldiers also take any photos they find that show the women. One elderly soldier with a grey moustache says to Erika, 'At home I'm going to tell everyone that you are my wife!'

The two soldiers then make a show of the watches they have taken. The elderly one has ten watches of all shapes and sizes around his right arm. The officer comes to the basement door and shouts, 'All out!'

Erika sighs, relieved. 'That's it, we're going home.'

But once outside, they're disappointed. They are not allowed to go home, but are marched further east again. Hope vanishes, and Cilly asks herself when the endless marching will stop. She's been gone from the farm for three days already, so when will they finally reach their destination so she can start working and then go home again? Most women are crying silently while they walk, but no one dares to say a word. This time their march is a short one – after 30 minutes they stop in another part of town in front of a church. Cilly is elated, thinking they are being given a chance to rest and pray, even though soldiers have brought a few coats and some goats to a spot in front of the church, where the goats are slaughtered. Once she steps into the half-light inside the church though, she can't believe her eyes. The church is filled with men and women, all in civilian clothes, sitting and lying on the benches and on the dirty floor, some with bloody and dirty dressings, all companions in misfortune. The scene is eerie and horrible enough on account of the ragged prisoners alone, but there's fire burning too: the Russians have made a fire in the pulpit to warm themselves, and even the wooden boards with psalms for the Sunday service have been ripped from the walls and thrown into the pulpit, God's words being fed to the fire. In every corner there's a stove on which something is being cooked by Red Army men. Smoke and the smell of frying meat fill the church. Russian soldiers are riding bikes up and down the aisles, laughing and shouting. Cilly has not cried all week, but now her right hand automatically makes the sign of the cross and then grasps the small silver crucifix she's wearing around her neck. She starts sobbing.

~

That crucifix she's wearing: I have it now. The only tangible item that I know went with Cilly to Russia and came back with her is her crucifix. It is nothing special. A small, black-and-silver one, made from some sort of metal. If it is tarnished silver, I cannot say. On the back there's an inscription: For Your 1st Holy Communion. Cilly was Catholic, a rarity in predominately Protestant East Prussia, a religion she had inherited from her pious father. She must have been given the crucifix when she was nine, in 1932, even before East Prussia became part of Nazi Germany. And it meant so much to her that she carried it with her to Russia and back, and bequeathed it to her son in her will. Now it is sitting on my desk, and it went to Russia and back with me as well.

I wonder how she kept it safe. Russian soldiers and guards made their prisoners hand over any precious items (or items perceived to be precious) – from watches and jewellery in East Prussia to combs and shoes during bathhouse stops en route to the camps and in the camp itself. Guards stole from them and fellow inmates stole from them. And yet, Cilly managed to hide that little piece of belief and home.

Depending on the camp she was in and the fierceness of the guards, discovery of the crucifix and the ensuing punishment could have killed her, even if she wasn't sentenced to death. But she was stubborn and would not give it up – for which I admire her. After she returned from the East she bequeathed it to her son, who in turn gave it to me. I put it on the day I left for Poland and Russia, and it became one of the talismans of my trip into the past.

~

Cilly pulls herself together, her hand still clutching the crucifix. She can smell food, which is dished out to the prisoners at the church. The meat of the animals slaughtered outside is distributed to the cooking fires inside, where prisoners queue for stew. Cilly learns another thing: if you don't have a container for your food, you go hungry. The Russian cooks have no crockery to give out, so empty-handed prisoners are just shooed away and have to wait for a good-hearted fellow prisoner to lend them their bowl after finishing.

Cilly spends two nights in the church, and then again there's the order of 'All out!' Outside the door, a group of officers stare at the coughing and blinking prisoners as they emerge from the church, taking in the dishevelled state of the women with bulging eyes. Cilly cannot say if they are shocked or amused. It takes the guards hours to count everyone, the warmth from inside the church evaporating quickly as the prisoners stand shivering in the cold. Frozen to the marrow in temperatures of minus 20 degrees, they are marched further east, past smoking rubble and snow-covered woods. Again, there are corpses in the gutters.

Now, after a night in the warmth of the church and witnessing the scenes inside, there is a lot of crying among the women, desperation properly setting in for the first time. Cilly lets the tears run down onto her lips to moisten them a little. For hours and hours they march, their ankles and knees hurting so much they can only move forwards sluggishly. In the evening they arrive at another town in ruins. They have reached Insterburg.

Insterburg had been an important provincial town with 50,000 inhabitants before the war. When the prisoners arrive, only 8,000 people remain. A large Soviet air attack destroyed most of the town before the arrival of the Red Army, and when it was taken on 22 January 1945, the NKVD immediately set up a large internment camp around the city prison. The prison itself had not been emptied by the Soviet authorities, so the women have to share their space with criminals and captured German soldiers. The conditions are worse than in Heilsberg. The prison and surrounding barracks are crammed, and no medical supplies are available. In February and March 1945, between 30 and 35 people die here each day, from dysentery, pneumonia, dystrophy, spotted fever, and injuries sustained during fighting or the transport.

They arrive filthy and emaciated. The first thing Cilly sees as her column marches into the large yard is an old man sitting on the ground, leaning against the wall right next to the entrance gate, his clothes in tatters. A Russian soldier curses and hits him on the head with the butt of his rifle and the man silently sinks to the ground, limp as a sack of flour. Cilly is too tired to feel anything. They have to stand to attention in the yard for another roll call, before being herded into a large hall, where about 200 captives are already spread out around the room, and everyone tries to get hold of a small piece of ground to lie or at least sit on. It looks like the former pigsty and abattoir of the prison: there are pig gates along one side of the room. Cilly has lost Erika. When they reached the prison, she was marched off to another area. Among the many dirty faces, she sees a few that seem somewhat familiar, but so far there are no other women from Lengainen. It is so crowded that nobody can lie down properly. Nevertheless, she falls asleep, leaning against strangers.

The conditions in the camp: twice a day the prisoners are brought to a large lavatory pit, the guards sneering at them while they defecate next to each other.

On the way to the latrine, the Russians have erected a banner with the slogan 'To the Führer's Mass'. In their quarter is a steel drum for the same purpose, but prisoners cannot get there without stepping on somebody. Cilly has not properly brushed her teeth for over a week now, only using her fingers or twigs as a makeshift toothbrush, nor has she washed her body or face. There's no running water anywhere in the camp, and the only liquid they see is the thin soup they receive for lunch, together with a scoop of water and, when they're lucky, hard pieces of rye bread that no one can break or chew. The corners of her mouth crack as she tries to moisten the bread. Her mouth feels unclean and her breath is vile, and this is the

8 *Souvenir photo of unknown friend, Soviet Union, 1940s*

first time, after a week of marching, that she can take stock of herself and realise how dirty everyone is and how bad she smells. They get hungrier every day. The prisoners are quarrelling and small fights break out, everyone trying to protect their belongings. Cilly is constantly keeping an eye on her little bag with her spare clothes and the few morsels of cheese and ham, and she sits on it at night. On the third day, as she returns from the lavatory pit, the pigsty is even more crowded than usual – it seems the Russians have shoved in another group of prisoners. Right next to Cilly's spot, with her back to the wall, sits a small elderly woman with long grey hair in thick braids, wearing a worn brown coat. She looks at Cilly, shuffles back and nods at the space she has created. 'Want to squeeze in? Sit down. My name is Angelika.'

~

I have made Angelika up. I know that Cilly had friends and comrades in the camps. She once showed me a stitched cloth greeting card that someone had made for her birthday in 1948, and among her photo albums there's a picture of a stocky woman in a dark dress, framed by a paper mount with painted angels, flowers and drapes, and in the bottom left corner are the words, in Russian, 'For Memory'. 'Mary Studtfeldt in Russia', it says in German on the back. What connection Cilly had to this woman, what happened to her and where she is today I don't know – and that goes for all the friends Cilly had in the camps. So I decided to invent one.

4 INTERMISSION: A LONG ACCOUNT OF CALAMITIES

The Warsaw Uprising

Sometimes, the world is as small as an anthill, so that one properly loses the respect for it; and the shadows of things long gone are so big that one can't escape and is constantly hounded by them.

Joseph Roth, *Das Leben ist ein Wartesaal*

I step into the car and drive away from the petrol station, leaving the Olsztyn suburbs behind in the sunshine, and plunge into the deep, shady woods that line the motorway. I put my foot down and aim for Warsaw: I have three hours left before the rental company starts charging for an additional day. In two days, my train leaves Warsaw for Moscow. There are no direct trains from Insterburg, or Chernyakhovsk in the Russian Kaliningrad Oblast today, to Moscow, so to emulate Cilly's journey I need to make a detour via the Polish capital.

I had said goodbye to Allenstein and Olsztyn the day before and driven to Lengainen again. This time I had parked at the lake, left the car and in the last rays of the sinking sun walked to the shore. I had stooped down and scratched some of the earth from the lakeside into two small laminated cardboard boxes bought earlier in the day. Then I had gone back to the car and driven to Olsztyn for a last drink in Pozytywka.

I zip down the motorway, overtaking slower cars and trucks while laughing at the gods of delay and accident. A week and a half in rural Poland, and I am driving like a local. Polish reggae band ComeYah are blasting from the car stereo, the sun is shining and, thanks to a bank holiday, the roads are relatively empty and I make good progress.

At another petrol station, I buy mineral water and a sandwich. While I'm walking back to the car, I hear a sound reminiscent of a marching drum, playing a slow, steady beat. Boom. Boom. Boom. I walk past the shop to the area where buses and trucks park and witness a strange spectacle. A group of teenagers and children is marching in formation, with a middle-aged man standing at the centre of three interweaving circles of children. He is solemnly beating a drum strapped to his waist. No one says a word, no one smiles. Everyone is wearing their everyday clothes, red and green Pokémon shirts and shorts and skirts, and the children turn and form fresh circles at preordained times without uttering a word or changing their facial expressions. I'm the only spectator, so I watch the spectacle for another minute or so and walk back to the car. It looks like a rehearsal for a marching display of sorts, and a martial one at that. I wonder what the bank holiday is about.

I have another hour before I reach the Polish capital, and that gives me time to think. Cilly was always a dominating presence in my life, especially when I was growing up. My mother's parents lived in another part of Germany, and we only visited them for holidays and on special occasions. Cilly and Willy I visited often. After school, which was just around the corner from their house, I went there for lunch and spent the afternoon with them, before walking home or being picked up by my parents. It feels as if it was always Cilly who took care of me. Not that Willy never talked or played with me, but due to her restlessness if feels like it was always Cilly who took me on walks, played with me and read me stories. Maybe it was her physical presence that made her so dominant in my early years. She was constantly cuddling me, placing wet kisses on my forehead and cheeks, ruffling my hair while slipping sweets into the pockets of my coat. It was Cilly who made me the avid reader I am today. I started to read in Kindergarten when I was about five years old. I don't remember my first book, but I remember vividly how Cilly stimulated and motivated me to read. 'Just imagine how cosy it will be when you can read a book on your own. When it's raining outside you can sit on your bed with a glass of milk and a chocolate bar and read as many books as you want!' That image stayed with me and motivated me to learn to master reading as soon as possible. I still have the copy of my favourite novel, Alexandre Dumas' *Three Musketeers*, which she gave me for Christmas when I was nine years old, with her scrawled dedication: Your grandparents, Christmas 1986.

Maybe because of my reminiscing, or maybe because I feel that I discovered the first piece of the puzzle in Olsztyn, Allenstein, Łęgajny and Lengainen, my spirits are high until I reach the outskirts of Warsaw and promptly get stuck in traffic. One lane of the motorway is closed for construction work. My rental car does not have a navigation system, so I have to rely on my printed-out Google maps and a street atlas. When I reach central Warsaw, I promptly get lost: the hotel is close to the massive hulk of the Palace of Culture and Science and I can see that landmark from the road, but I have to return the car at the Marriott hotel on the other side of the palace. I misread the map, drive across the large white Józef Poniatowski bridge and the Vistula, need to make a U-turn over five lanes of traffic and promptly drive past the Marriott, only to identify it too late and drive another 2 kilometres before I have the chance to make another turn across tram tracks and three more lanes. I park at the designated car park 15 minutes late and with smoking tyres, and hasten through the massive lobby until I finally find the rental company desk where a little round woman smiles at me and says: 'Welcome to Warsaw!'

It's three in the afternoon and I need a beer. Thankfully I don't need to pay the extra charge.

My hotel is right in the middle of the socialist array of concrete high-rise buildings behind Marszałkowska Street. Walking over from the Marriott, I'm not overly impressed by Warsaw: its cracked pavements, screaming tacky adverts everywhere, stifling inner-city summer heat and the absence of any green spaces. There are a few dried-out lawns and lonely trees in front of the massive tower of the Palace of Culture and Science, Stalin's 'present' from 1955 that dwarfs every other building around. After I've left the crowded shopping areas, the tall buildings provide shade, and suddenly there's something appealing about the concrete landscape of the Polish capital, the smell of a proper city in summer. I feel I have adjusted to the country and its language enough that I no longer feel like an idiot stumbling around asking the wrong questions.

There's another thing about Warsaw: on every street corner, there are plaques, some bigger, some smaller. Most of them carry a small sign that looks like an anchor, made from the words 'p' and 'w'. Some of the signs are old and made from rusting metal, some are newer and made from plastic, but all seem to have been adorned with wreaths and candles in the last days. The flowers still look fresh and the candles haven't completely melted despite the summer heat.

My hotel is a beige behemoth from the 1970s, with over 1,000 rooms and no air conditioning. My room on the fourth floor looks at the opposite wing of the hotel and nothing else. The heat has become unbearable. It feels like a wet bell jar has been put over Warsaw and there's almost no oxygen left. Every movement covers me in sweat, and just unpacking my bag induces the need to change my shirt.

While I'm unpacking, something strange happens. It is around five in the afternoon when suddenly a loud wail erupts, the rising and falling howl of an air-raid siren, a sound I haven't heard since my childhood in the '80s. But why here, why today? I suspect it to be an exercise, but for a split second there's the childish fear that the sound of an air-raid siren always evokes in me – what if this is the real thing? Will there suddenly be vapour trails of jets appearing in the sky, and after

9 *Armia Krajowa memorial, Warsaw*

a moment everything disappearing in the blinding melting
heat of an atomic explosion? I shake my head to dispel these
images and crane my head out of the window, to look down to
the street on the left. I witness something extraordinary: all the
passers-by have stopped. Some of them are standing directly in
the blinding sunshine, some in the shade of the hotel, and even
the taxi driver unloading his trunk has seemingly stopped mid-
movement and stands to attention; some bags and suitcases of
the confused-looking tourist family standing next to him are

still in the trunk, some on the ground next to the similarly frozen page boy. The howling goes on for a few more seconds, and then abruptly stops. Everyone resumes their activities, and I wonder if the heat has finally gotten to me and I imagined all this.

'Have you seen what the people did when the sirens sounded?' Stephan asks.

Two days later, I am sitting in a hip cafe off Chlodna Street, the road that used to divide the Warsaw Ghetto between 1940 and 1945. I'm right next to where the wooden bridge between the two parts of the ghetto had been. Today there's nothing left except a few metal bands inserted in the asphalt symbolising the two walls of the ghetto, and a small monument with old photographs of the same street corner 70 years ago. Stephan is a lanky Polish photographer in his twenties who lives in Warsaw and who has travelled to Russia; this is why we're meeting today. The fact that Stephan is a local Warsaw expert will also help me to understand the city better, I hope.

'We do it to remember and commemorate the exact date and time when the Warsaw Uprising started in 1944 – at 5 o'clock on August 1st. It is called W-hour, from the Polish word for explosion or fight. Everyone observes a minute of silence and stands to attention when the sirens sound.'

The Warsaw Uprising was the final major operation by the Polish Resistance Home Army, the *Armia Krajowa*, and the last attempt to liberate Warsaw from Nazi Germany before the Red Army arrived. However, the Soviet advance stopped short, enabling the Germans to regroup and defeat the Polish resistance, which fought for 63 days with little outside support, neighbourhood for neighbourhood, block for block, house for house. The Uprising was the largest single military effort undertaken by any European resistance movement of World War II. When it began, the main Polish objectives were to drive the German occupiers from the city and to underscore the sovereignty of the pre-war Polish Republic by empowering the

Polish Underground State and its armed forces before the So-
viet-backed Polish Committee of National Liberation could assume control of the country. Initially, the Polish fighters established control over most of central Warsaw, but the Soviets ig-
nored Polish attempts to establish radio contact and did not
advance beyond the city limits. This, along with the lack of Soviet air support, led to allegations that Stalin deliberately halted
his forces to allow the Polish insurrectionists to be crushed by
the Germans. Winston Churchill also pleaded with Stalin and
Franklin D. Roosevelt to help Britain's Polish allies, to no avail.
Then, without Soviet air clearance, Churchill decided to send
the Royal Air Force to drop supplies. The Soviet Union refused
to allow Allied bombers from Western Europe to land on Soviet airfields after dropping supplies to the Poles, so the RAF
pilots had to make a 2,600-kilometre round trip to reach Warsaw from their Italian airfields. Despite the air support from
the western Allies, the Home Army forces surrendered on 2
October 1944.

About 16,000 members of the Polish resistance were killed,
and between 150,000 and 200,000 Polish civilians died, many
from mass executions carried out by German punishment battalions and the SS. During the street fighting, approximately 25
per cent of Warsaw was destroyed. Following the surrender
and a personal order of SS chief Heinrich Himmler, German
troops systematically destroyed another 35 per cent of the city,
often with the help of flamethrowers, block by block. After this
and the earlier damage during the invasion of Poland in 1939
and the Ghetto Uprising of 1943, over 85 per cent of the city
lay in ruins by January 1945, when the Germans finally abandoned the city.

'After the Uprising, Warsaw was almost deserted, as the
Germans also deported most inhabitants. But some people hid
in the deserted city,' says Stephan. 'They were called "Robinson
Crusoes" or "cavemen". The best-known Robinson Crusoe in
Warsaw was Władysław Szpilman, whose memoir *The Pianist*

was adapted into a successful movie. And now look at the city today. Would you think all this is just 70 years old?'

My answer is no, and I am suddenly amazed by this city, which refused to die. After saying goodbye to Stephan and walking through the former ghetto and past the only structure from that time left standing, a pockmarked brown building decorated with large black-and-white images of the former inhabitants, I realise that in Warsaw the dead are everywhere. On street corners, in parks and in mass graves, long buried under apartment blocks and skyscrapers. Besides the countless little plaques and memorials I noticed earlier, the most spine-chilling things I encounter are the fresh graffiti of the *kotwica*, the anchor emblem used by the Polish resistance. Some are on newer buildings seemingly unconnected to the Uprising, some close to memorials. It looks as if the dead fighters have risen as ghosts to paint them overnight, reminding me not to forget them.

The next morning, after squishy scrambled eggs served in a windowless breakfast room in the basement of my hotel, I walk to the Old Town. In front of the castle, the city authorities have set up a water hose to cool down the cobblestones in front of the main entrance, and giggling tourists (including me) walk through the rainbow fountain created by the spewing water. The Old Town is pleasant, and fake. The city of Warsaw was rebuilt, with the Old Town thoroughly reconstructed. But, as in Gdansk and Olsztyn, the destruction of the inner city was so severe that in order to rebuild the older parts of Warsaw, an eighteenth-century landscape painting by Italian artists Marcello Bacciarelli and Bernardo Bellotto had to be used to recreate most of the buildings. Today there's shade in between the new old buildings, and the first tourists have already started drinking beer on the main square.

Maybe it is the omnipresence of the Warsaw Uprising that influences my view of the city. Living in Berlin, I am used to being confronted with World War II and Cold War history every day. Berlin, however, seems to remember the past in a centralised way: there's the Holocaust memorial, the memorial to the resistance against Hitler and so forth. In Warsaw, memorials to fallen soldiers are on every street corner, little badges indicating the names of the fighters and their units and the course of their actions, all adorned with candles, flags and flowers. I have underestimated the influence of the Uprising, but to understand it I don't need to look at images of fighting soldiers, their faces smeared with dirt and gun oil, aiming their machine guns over rubble at the encroaching Wehrmacht and the bastard Nazi party units of *Waffen-SS* and *Sonderdienst* and *Sonderabteilungen*. I just need to look at the weapons.

The Polish Home Army used a weapon made from scrap metal and hope: the *Błyskawica*. In 1942, engineer Wacław Zawrotny came up with the design for a cheap, homemade machine pistol to be used by the Polish resistance. Its main feature was its simplicity: it could be made in small workshops by inexperienced workers who had never assembled weapons before. The design was based on two of the most popular machine pistols of the era. The external construction, with a retractable butt and magazine mounted below the barrel, was borrowed from the German MP-40 while the internal design was modelled on the British Sten. The Poles also designed the weapon this way so that insurgents could restock their ammunition from captured German MP-40s. In the harsh conditions of German-occupied Warsaw, there were tight controls over the activity of repair shops, shortages of cutting tools, and rationing of suitable materials, which were put on a 'restricted supplies' list and sold only to permit holders. This made gathering the material for a prototype a very hard task. Nevertheless, bribing and stealing their way along and working by night in Zawrotny's flat, by early September 1943 the engineers had managed to manufacture and assemble the first working model.

The name *Błyskawica* came from the three lightning bolts

carved into the aluminium butt-plate. The name was made official in November, when the first batch of five guns was accepted by Home Army Command.

To avoid compromising the entire weapons programme in case the Germans should discover one main workshop, parts were produced by over 20 manufacturers scattered throughout the city, with a chicken-wire factory tasked with the final assembly and testing. The clandestine plant was situated under the legal workshop, in the cellars of the nearby Roman Catholic Church of All Saints. An additional concrete-lined tunnel acted as an underground shooting range. Test-firing the guns was performed strictly during rush hour to cover the noise.

Before the Uprising, roughly 600 guns were built, with an additional 40 during the fighting. In the end, the design proved very successful for urban combat. It was the only weapon designed and mass-produced covertly by any resistance movement in occupied Europe.

The Germans, on the other hand, used a gun that was so big it had a first name. Its shells weighed 2 tonnes. *Karl-Gerät*, the Karl device, was a self-propelled siege mortar, and the largest self-propelled weapon to see service in World War II. Its heaviest munition was a 60 cm diameter, 2,170 kg shell, and the range for its lightest shell of 1,250 kg was just over 10 km. Each gun had to be accompanied by a crane, a heavy transport trailer, and several modified tanks to carry the shells. It was also used to grind the city of Warsaw into rubble, on the personal order of the Führer. On 13 August 1944, a 54 cm Karl-Gerät was sent to the 9th Army to help it suppress the Warsaw Uprising. It arrived at the Warsaw West train station at 7 a.m. on 17 August 1944, although the ammunition train didn't arrive until the following morning. This was *Ziu*, and it started to pound the burning city the next day.

On 24 August the high command of the Wehrmacht noted that it had been very successful in combat and ordered another *Karl-Gerät* sent to Warsaw, with a third shipped there on 10

September. On 2 October 1944, the remaining Polish fighters capitulated in the rubble of their capital. At the Warsaw Uprising museum there is a colour photograph of one of those shells hitting a Polish-held skyscraper in the centre of the city. It looks like the World Trade Center collapsing upwards.

Whereas Berlin is shaped by multiple layers of recent history and events, everything in Warsaw today originates from this watershed moment, and the effect on a free people of seeing their city reduced to ruin. It is a tragic and at the same time extremely valiant act that shapes the city like no other event in its history. If the sound of Berlin is thudding techno played in stinking underground clubs, the sound of Warsaw is a melancholic Chopin piece.

I like it here. On my last evening in Poland, I decide to celebrate. For dinner I have *pirogi ruskie*, Polish dumplings filled with cheese and potatoes, in a *bar leczny*, or milk bar. Milk bars are a legacy from Communist times, small cafes that used to sell state-subsidised, mostly dairy-based and vegetarian meals, especially during the period of martial law in the early 1980s when meat was rationed. Most of them are gone now, but some have been privatised and still sell cheap, hearty fare. The one I'm in is airy and bright, and despite the lack of air conditioning not too hot, and I enjoy my plate of dumplings doused in butter and sour cream while listening to the chatter of the other customers without understanding anything. After my meal, I walk up the Golden Mile in the direction of the Old Town again, and stop at Przekąski Zakąski, a 24-hour bar. It is dominated by one large counter and a few stools dotted around the one room, and only serves one sort of beer (two euros), vodka (one euro) and snacks such as cucumber, bread and cold meats (I'm not hungry). I buy a vodka and beer chaser, sit down on one of the bar stools and turn around. I toast the sun setting over the fake Old Town of Warsaw, visible through the open bar door, and down the vodka. On the wall of the building opposite, someone has stuck a replica of a Polish propaganda poster printed during the Uprising. It depicts a skull wearing a German steel helmet under the slogan: 'One Bullet, One German'.

5 TRAINS

On the train: staring hypnotised at the blackness outside the window, feeling the incomparable rhythmic language of the wheels, clacking out nursery rhymes, summing up moments of the mind like the chant of a broken record: god is dead, god is dead. going, going, going.

Sylvia Plath, *The Unabridged Journals of Sylvia Plath*

I am ready to take the train to Russia. With no hangover and feeling surprisingly refreshed, I say goodbye to Warsaw the next morning, and make it to the giant concrete bus stop of Warsaw central station just in time to catch my train. The shady, grey-and-white '70s interior of Warsaw's underground main station cools the sweat running down my back, and I hope I don't get a cold.

Cilly was always fussing about me – dark rings under my fingernails meant vitamin deficiencies, and I was never dressed warmly enough for her when I was heading out to play, even in summer. I also wondered what trains meant for her. In Solingen, when we were travelling together we mostly walked, or took the bus, or my dad drove us around in his car. Train travel is my favourite mode of transport. For Cilly it must have meant something else, maybe just the average way of getting around, maybe something she always connected with her journey to Russia and back. Whatever way, she took the train regularly in later life. With joy, sometimes.

I'm still suffering from the intense August heat, and the forecast for Russia I looked up online promises no relief. I sit down on my bag on the platform, together with a mixed group of travellers: a school class on excursion, a Gypsy family with a vast array of bags and suitcases, women in high heels and short white dresses, and bald men in white polo shirts and tight jeans. I wonder what my compartment companions will look like. There will be either three or four bunks in my compartment, depending on whether it's a Polish or Russian train.

It seems to me that, in our time and age, we have lost the art of travel. No longer does it mean conviction and an acceptance that there is a distance between point of origin and destination. Instead, it has become an inconvenience, transit time between home and the selfie on the beach or by the pool. We are hardly ever concerned with the present, only living for what is to come and how we can best document it for our social media followers. Friends we have long left behind. The antidote, to my mind at least, is to take the train – and especially the night train. This is our chance to reconnect with the pres-

10   Cilly on the train, 1980s

ent, to enjoy the art of the journey as much as the destination. It is a deceleration express. Rather than sipping lukewarm beer while strapped into a flying tube, we can bring our own wine, or take a walk to the dining car and chat with like-minded passengers. We can watch the sun setting over the Hungarian Puszta, or let the clack-clacking of the train rock us gently to sleep before we see the sun rise over the Carpathian Mountains.

The night train is, and remains, the budget airline of the flâneurs, the idlers and the romantics. To my mind, sleeper trains also represent the best of the European project, connecting countries as they move through the night, all the while providing stories and memories that planes and airports just cannot compete with. And in the end, the night train is all about the journey. It is about late-night conversations in the bar, or the bleary-eyed early-morning views through the window. It is the stories contained in those carriages and compartments.

When the blue train of Polish Railways, PKP, pulls into the station and opens its doors, there's a bit of fairly hectic pushing and shoving as everyone tries to find the right compartment. The interior of my carriage is composed of a long corridor with windows and white-grey walls to the left, and six small compartments with three bunks on top of one another on the right-hand side. The bottom bunk has been folded away into a bench, and there's a small table by the window. I store my bag and rucksack beneath the bunk and look around. The hectic to and fro has abated, the train has started moving and so far no other travellers have entered the compartment. As I step outside to film us crossing the Vistula, an elderly couple shuffle past me and into the compartment, storing their bags and suitcases on the middle bunk and beneath the table. She is a round woman with a wide skirt, a blue blouse and long grey-blonde hair pulled into a bun; he's a lanky gentleman with glasses, white hair and a light-beige summer suit. We say hi in Polish, and I try further advances in English without success. German, however, leads to an affirmative smile and nodding.

'Nice to meet you, young man. I'm Dr Maria Szamborski and I and my husband Rafael are on our way to Moscow to meet friends for a summer holiday.'

We strike up a conversation. Both worked at the University of Kraków, but are now retired. She studied in Moscow in the 1960s, and they are on an annual trip to visit Russian friends and make a stopover in Lviv, where their family originally comes from and where all their parents are buried. As I tell them about my trip and Cilly, they don't bat an eyelid.

'Everyone who lived through Communist times knows that people have been moved, often forcibly, all over the place. Also by the Nazis. Just look at the place where my family comes from,' 'Frau' Szamborski says.

'The city of Lwów, Polish before World War II, for example, was occupied twice by the Red Army and once by the Wehrmacht. After the war ended it was called Lviv, not Lwów, and was no longer in eastern Poland but in the western part of Soviet Ukraine, and its Polish and Jewish pre-war population had been murdered by the Germans or deported and replaced by Ukrainians from the surrounding countryside. You will find many more traces of people from all over Europe the further you go east. Will you excuse me for a moment?'

While we men leave the compartment for a short while, the doctor puts on a more comfortable T-shirt and slippers, and then she and her husband sit down and open a can of beer. I squeeze into my corner of the bench and take a sip from my water bottle.

～

In 1945, during winter and war, Cilly, Angelika and most of the other prisoners in the pigsty are woken up by loud shouting one morning. 'All out for the roll call!' They shuffle out and form ranks in the prison yard, and reading their names takes hours. The guards use the Russian form, adding a -*kaya* to the end of the last names, so most women have no idea when to respond. The guards use old wooden calculators with wooden balls to check the number of prisoners, just like the one Cilly played with as a child. After the roll call, they are marched down Theatre Street, machine guns always aimed directly at them. Mountains of rubble cover the pavement and one side of the street. Insterburg Castle, once a proud fortress overlooking the town, is only recognisable by its foundation wall. At the station, a Russian train with over 40 carriages awaits the prisoners. The empty wagons are for cattle, not human beings, but some have a small stove in the centre for heating, and some have bunks in the form of one simple layer of planks, chest-high, without any bedding or even straw. That way more people fit into the wagons – if they're lucky, between 45 and 50 people per carriage, and if not, between 60 and 70 with no space to lie down. Cilly is lucky. The wagons have 'toilets', holes or drains in one corner for all sanitary needs and a large tin bucket to collect drinking water. There's also one small barred window directly beneath the carriage roof.

Men and women are separated, and Cilly is herded into one of the wagons together with other women to the shouts of '*Dawai, dawai, bistra!*' from the Russian guards. They shuffle around, each trying to find a place to lie or sit down, those with acquaintances and comrades hunkering down in pairs and groups. Cilly sits with Angelika. Do they still think that they are being taken to work somewhere in East Prussia? Or has it dawned on them that they have been abducted? One thing is sure: when the sliding doors close on the wagon, each and every one of the women feels a connection severed, to their home, their land, their family. A loud wailing and crying breaks out, from women longing for the children they have been forced to leave behind, for their families, their friends. They have seen death before: dead soldiers during their flight, the frozen corpses next to the hospital in Mohrungen, women and children dead from sickness and starvation in Insterburg. Do they sense that some of their fellow captives will not see the end of the trip? Do they cry and scratch at the carriage wall, or do they hug their knees, their gaze without focus, waiting for whatever will come?

The women in the carriage come from all walks of life: feisty farm girls like Cilly, merchants' daughters from Allenstein and Insterburg, the wives of carpenters and butchers and publicans, officers' darlings and spinsters with grey hair. They are 17, 48, 29, 38, 54, 22.

Cilly has a distinctive advantage: she is used to hard physical work, and also still has some of the food she took from the farm, which she shares with the women around her once the train starts moving. They don't know that the real torment has not yet started. Once a day, the train stops and the prisoners receive their rations: an armful of birch wood for the stove and food. A prisoner's regular dry ration for the trip consists of bread, mostly rye bread, which is distributed either in small chunks of 300 g a day, or else in larger quantities – 2 kg or so – meant to last a 34-day journey. Along with the bread, prisoners are sometimes given salted fish, the effect of which is to make them extremely thirsty, but they are rarely given more than one mug of water per day, or sometimes a pail of water is splashed into the tin bucket next to the stove. This is the standard rationing on Soviet prisoner transports. The effect, however, is the same as deliberate torture. On some journeys there are no provisions for three to four days, forcing the women to break off the black icicles hanging from the window, stained by the dirt of the journey and the soot from the locomotive, and suck on them.

The sanitary conditions are horrifying to the women, who are embarrassed at having to urinate and defecate in front of one another. Some women also mistake the food and water bucket for chamber pots on the first days of the journey – sometimes they're lucky and the Russians replace them, some times they have to use the soiled container for the rest of the trip. With not enough water to wash away the faeces from the drain, and only water and coarse rye bread as provisions, dysentery is soon in every carriage. Those women who use the drain often unwillingly splash those sitting nearest to the 'toilet' with urine and faeces.

Once a day, the train stops, the carriage doors are opened up; provisions go in and corpses come out. On the prisoner transports in early 1945, between 30 and 50 per cent of the prisoners die during the two- to four-week-long journey, some of dysentery, some of exhaustion and some of despair. There are young mothers who have left their children behind, pregnant women, girls just in their teens, all ripped from their lives and put into a black train travelling through winter. Sometimes the dead bodies are stacked in an empty carriage at the end of the train, so that the bodies on the train still match the prisoner list, while at other times the corpses are just thrown down the railroad embankment or buried in shallow graves scratched into the frozen ground.

During the journey, the women stand on their toes to peep out of the small window in the wagon door at the passing land, but whenever the train stops the guards start shouting and raise their guns to drive the women away. Sometimes, the women think they know where they are. Some might have been this way before. But things have changed over the past few years in these parts of Poland and Ukraine. The women see villages in ruins, dynamited factories and areas now bleak and devoid of life where the orders were to burn even the few remaining trees. So perhaps they recognise nothing. Perhaps they think they are entering the land of the dead...

~

I'm sitting in a nice compartment with pleasant travel companions, the sinking summer sun shining through the window and with refreshments at the ready; even complimentary water provided by Polish Railways PKP. Cilly also had complimentary water and bread, but only once a day. Nothing else. Like me, she didn't choose her travel companions – but where I have two, she had 50 in a cattle wagon. I have my own bunk, complete with bed linen. But the most important difference, I think, is that I know where I'm going and I can get off any time I want. I decide not to visit the restaurant car, and continue munching the rye bread I bought in Warsaw. The *provodnitsa*, or conductress, who also looks after providing bed linen and hot water for tea and who sells snacks and drinks from her little compartment at the end of the carriage, has already sold me a non-alcoholic beer, the only type of beer on board my train.

We cross the River Bug as the sun sets, and I step outside into the corridor to take a few pictures, the clack-clack, clack-clack of the train providing the soundtrack to the gently flowing river which mirrors the red sky. The dark orange bowl of the sun is framed by the green trees which overhang the banks and a grey metal bridge in the distance. The train is going at exactly the right speed, fast enough to convey a sense of making progress, but still slow enough for me to take in the scenery outside the windows.

After an hour or so we stop at the border with Belarus, at a small station in the middle of nowhere, consisting of a few crumbling sheds surrounded by dry grassland. Polish border guards in blue uniforms enter the train, check our passports and then leave again. Standing on the border of one of the few socialist dictatorships left in Europe, I am hoping for more Cold War seriousness, but the young Polish border guards are friendly and laugh with the backpackers in the next compartment, who seem to have taken the wrong train and leave together with the guards. Our train then slowly inches forwards, eastwards. We drive through what looks like an abandoned business park, then after another five minutes or so we stop again, at another small station with a similar look. This time,

Belorussian border guards come aboard, and I finally get what I am looking for: men in ill-fitting green-and-brown uniforms and hats adorned with impressive red-and-green badges stare at me over the edge of my passport, wordlessly handing it to the *provodnitsa* and pushing an immigration form in my face. Together with the Szamborskis I hunch over the forms, scribbling down my details using a book to lean on as the train jerks and starts moving again. Are they keeping my passport?

'No worries – Belarus shares the border controls with Russia, so the *provodnitsa* will hand you back your passport shortly before Moscow,' Dr Szamborski explains.

'You just hand in the first form and keep the second copy until you leave Russia – then you hand it in at border control again. All very socialist, isn't it?'

I exhale and lean back as we slowly travel on, this time over a field of tracks into what looks like a very long hangar.

'Ah, this will interest you. They're changing the wheels!'

In 1842, the so-called 'Russian gauge' of 1,524 mm was approved as the standard for railway track in Czarist Russia. Many believe the choice was made for military reasons, to prevent potential invaders from using the Russian rail system. George Washington Whistler, the American railway engineer hired as a consultant by the Czar for the building of Russia's first major railway on the Moscow to St Petersburg line, was a proponent of a wider gauge and lobbied for the new standard, which was subsequently introduced all over the empire. Today, Russia and most of the former Russian Empire (including the Baltic States, Ukraine, Belarus, the Caucasian and Central Asian republics) have the Russian gauge track. And this is why my train to Moscow needs to be lifted from the ground. The long hangar we have rolled into looks like any other factory hall in the world, with dirty brown walls, long windows in the ceilings and machinery of different sorts scattered about. There's a long line of what look like yellow hydraulic elevators on each side of the train. Workers in grubby blue overalls descend beneath our carriage to unscrew the undercarriage, and after they reappear there's another jerk. One by one, the carriages are separated and the elevators placed beneath. After a while, it seems as if an invisible giant tugs at the wheels of our train, and while we float in the air in our now wheel-less carriages, the wheels and axles roll away from under us. Clack-clack, clack-clack, clack-clack.

~

There is no stop to change the gauge on Cilly's train. Or if there is one, the women in the dark car don't realise. Their train stops every few hours for no discernible reason, and for them it would have been just one stop among many others. It's possible that they're already travelling on the Russian gauge. The Germans destroyed the train tracks during their retreat, using a device called a *Schienenwolf,* or track wolf; a long steel hook attached to the last wagon of the last train retreating before the Red Army, which ripped the tracks in two. Soviet engineers had started building their own rail lines right behind the advancing army, and might have brought their own gauge with them to Insterburg.

After the first few hours on the train, most prisoners have settled into a stupor. Lulled by the clack-clack, clack-clack of the wheels, most of the women around Cilly have either fallen asleep or surrendered to their fate, staring into nothingness, some sniffing, and some silently crying. Those on board with friends or relatives huddle together, younger girls with their heads in the laps of older women. While it's still minus ten degrees Celsius outside, the packed humanity inside the carriage has at least some warmth. Soon the first hushed conversations will start: *Where are they taking us? Will they shoot us? Why are they taking us?* But not now. It's too dark to do anything anyway; the light which falls through the small window and creeps through the gaps between the wooden planks is slipping away. East they're going, east. Cilly nods off, leaning against Angelika. Outside, a snowstorm has started to rage, and when Cilly awakens the icy fingers of wind are driving through the thin wooden walls of the carriage. No sleep at all and then night becomes day again, and the trapped air around them is filled by the thickening stink of their own dirt, a reeking stench, all sweat and grime while excrement slops in brimming buckets. They cling to their bunks, weak against the white fury outside. Cilly lies there curling into her own body as if she could protect herself from the elements and the faraway people who seem to have plotted the downfall of every single woman in the carriage.

The train stutters to a halt, and the women sit up on their elbows as noises move down the train, coming close to their carriage. Shouts of *'Dawai, dawai!'* followed by more clanking noises and shuffling. And then suddenly the sliding door of their carriage is opened, and the grey and overcast light of the winter morning makes the women shield their eyes and blink.

'Three women out for carrying food!' shouts a black-haired female translator in a padded kilt, flanked by two Russian guards with submachine guns.

'Quick, quick!'

Two women grab the bucket and shuffle outside, followed by a third. A few minutes later, they are back and heave the bucket into the carriage, half-filled with steaming soup. The third woman, a lanky girl with huge glasses, puts three loaves of black bread and a smaller bucket filled with water next to it. For a moment, everyone stares at each other. Then the door is closed and everything becomes twilight again.

'Don't all go for the food at the same time!' Angelika shouts.

'Who has cups or any other container we could use to share the soup?'

A few arms are raised, and the women shuffle towards the bucket against the rocking of the train. Slowly, a few battered cups and mugs are handed around the carriage, until everyone has had their share of watery soup and bread and drinking water. Then they lean back, sinking into their stupor again. And the train goes clack-clack, clack-clack, clack-clack.

~

After the old wheels have been removed, another set of wider wheels is positioned under our carriage. We are lowered and the workers set to work, tightening screws with large electric screwdrivers and adjusting levers, until the elevators are pulled away, and the wagons are slowly pushed against each other until our train is complete again. We set off, away from the Belorussian hangar and further east. The heat has caught up with me, and I try as often as possible to get a whiff of fresh air from the open windows in the corridor, but there's no real relief.

It's shortly after nine in the evening when our train pulls into a station and we stop for a while. Nothing extraordinary to see here, no guards with Kalashnikovs and Alsatians patrol the platforms in front of the darkened and closed station building, only a group of teenagers loiters, the girls in insanely high heels and hot pants, the boys in white sneakers, tracksuit bottoms and white shirts. I turn away from the window and realise that the Szamborskis have started making their beds, leaving me the honour of the top bunk. After the couple has crawled off to bed and after some tooth-brushing shenanigans at the tiny washbasin, I finally manage to enter my bunk without breaking anything. I have about 30 cm of space and air above my head, and somehow manage to wiggle out of my shirt and to cover my lower parts with the flimsy blanket. I wonder if I'll melt away – the sweat just keeps pouring out of me. Clack-clack, clack-clack, clack-clack.

~

A few days later, the train suddenly stops outside the established schedule. Again the cries of '*Dawai! Dawai!*' coming down the train, but this time the guards seem to take longer than usual between the carriages. After a while their door is opened, and the translator shouts: 'Any dead? No? Good. All out!'

Cilly looks around at the other women curiously – have they reached their destination? Will they now find out what the Russians have planned for them? The women from Cilly's carriage are herded down the frozen railway embankment, and towards what looks like a small railway building with a few sheds attached, all covered in snow. There's steam coming from one of the sheds, and another group of prisoners passes them, their faces flushed red, as they are ushered back towards the train. Cilly's group is pushed towards one of the sheds, a flimsy construction of wooden planks and tar. They are each given a small sliver of soap and ordered to undress. Cilly is un-sure – are they really going to give them time to wash them-selves? Is it just a ruse to make them suffer even more? More cries of '*Dawai!*' emerge from the guards, and everyone starts to unbutton their blouses and skirts. After having to toss their belongings into the snow outside the hut, they march shivering towards the building which emanates steam, past a group of Red Army officers in long coats, who laughingly observe the passing women prisoners and remark on the state of their breasts and hips to each other. Inside, they find a few wooden tubs, half-filled with lukewarm water. Reluctantly, the women start to rub and scrub themselves with the coarse soap. The bath isn't fully heated and there are cracks in the wall. There are constant shouts from the guards to 'Hurry! Hurry!' After they're done, after what cannot have been more than 30 minutes, they are marched back again to the first hut, still drip-ping water from their hair. They are made to select their clothes again from a big damp heap of clothing (their clothes had been steamed in the meantime to delouse them) amidst shuffling and shouting. Some clothes and smaller items (a comb here, a brooch there) are missing and quite a few of the women end up with less clothing than before. Cilly asks the translator what has happened to the missing items, half-expecting a slap. 'These were all found to be infected during the delousing process and have been burned. Stop asking.'

The women are marched back to the train, away from the steaming sheds in the middle of nowhere, and packed back into their wagons.

'Well, that was something,' Angelika says to Cilly after everyone has settled back into their bunks and the train again shuffles on eastwards.

'That must have been the worst bath I have ever taken.'

~

Clack-clack, clack-clack, clack-clack. I awake, not quite as sweat-drenched as expected, to the sounds of the Szamborskis scrambling around the cabin beneath me. I'm not sure where we are, but the summer sun pours through the window and the sound of the train bears us further eastwards. I'm greeted with a friendly 'Guten Morgen!' as I swing myself down towards the floor, but I'm not yet ready for small talk and answer with a grunt. After another cat lick at the washbasin (by now I no longer really care about my smell and general appearance, maybe the first signs of travel weariness) I gladly accept a hot tea and a croissant wrapped in plastic that the Szamborskis have acquired for me from the *provodnitsa*. It seems that while I slept we entered Russia, without any additional border controls, and are slowly but surely approaching the outskirts of the Russian capital. Landscape-wise, it's more or less the same as eastern Poland. A flat country, lots of fields interspersed with a few run-down villages and the odd florid, Soviet-style train station. Again, I am surprised at how much the landscape here resembles both Poland and the area around Berlin. What was it that made people and nations fight over the same land for hundreds of years, in a landscape that seems interchangeable?

There are no mountain ranges, no river deltas, no large lakes here worthy of mention. Maybe it has always been just the dirt in the ground. Clack-clack, clack-clack, clack-clack.

~

Cilly's train crawls towards the rising sun. How long they're on the way, no one knows. There are a few other women on the train who speak and write Russian, and it's with these women that Cilly takes turns at the small window. They provide the rest of the passengers with information whenever they spot a train station sign or anything else that gives away where they are. Besides this, there's nothing to do except to hunt for lice – which are by now infesting the women – to talk and wait for the daily food ration. Some women are severely ill by now, mostly city girls suffering from dysentery. They have been moved closer to the 'toilet', so they don't have to walk too far and risk soiling the others.

Most days, they travel slowly under a low-hanging grey winter sky, through a landscape that looks devoid of life. Cilly sometimes spots a few groups of Russian peasants standing next to what look like holes in the ground which are emitting smoke from cooking fires. But besides some crudely and hastily built station buildings, a few burnt-out wrecks of tanks and lorries and buildings and factories, plus the odd soldiers' graveyard, there isn't much to see. They are going through an area that has seen the most brutal fighting of the war between Germany and Russia. Both nations applied a scorched earth policy here, when they were passing through on their advance and retreat and advance and retreat again.

~

As Anne Applebaum puts it in Iron Curtain: *The Crushing of Eastern Europe 1944–1956*:

During the war, Eastern Europe experienced the worst of both Hitler and Stalin's ideological madness. By 1945, most of the territory between Poznan in the west and Smolensk in the east was occupied not once but twice, or even three times. Following the Molotov-Ribbentrop Pact of 1939, Hitler invaded the region from the west, occupying western Poland. Stalin invaded from the east, occupying eastern Poland, the Baltic States and Bessarabia. In 1941, Hitler once again invaded these same territories from the west. In 1943, the tide turned and the Red Army marched back through the same region, coming from the east. So by 1945, the armies and secret police of not one, but two totalitarian states had marched through the region, each bringing profound ethnic and political changes.

～

The cold is getting worse and worse. Just a few metres away from the trickle of warmth coming from the oven, the upper part of the wall is covered in frost, the women's breath steaming towards the ceiling. Everyone is wrapped in as many layers of clothing as possible, hands hidden in armpits or in long sleeves. One morning, Cilly awakes with a start, only to realise her head is frozen to the wall. Luckily she is wearing her headscarf slung around her head to protect it from the cold, and no skin has been exposed to the frost.

At one stop, the translator and the guards throw a few rectangular packs of brown paper into the wagon. As the women peel these open, they're in for a surprise. 'Lard!' Angelika bursts out. Soon the women gather around the packages, and Angelika manages to somewhat evenly distribute a spoonful of lard to everyone. Clack-clack, clack-clack, clack-clack.

～

The rest of my journey to Moscow consists of passing a variety of flat country, lots of fields, a few rivers, all interspersed with a handful of villages and the odd train station. Closing in on Moscow, there are more and more buildings made from pre-cast concrete slabs, the *Plattenbauten* I know from Berlin, some dirty garages and some sad, weedy parks. Altogether the suburbs here remind me of Warsaw, just a bit more run-down – and the same applies to the bums in tracksuit trousers and white undershirts who jaywalk drunkenly between the train tracks and the running trains.

I step from the train together with the Szamborskis at *Belorusskaya*, the Belorussian station, one of the nine dead-end stations of Moscow. The heat is as bad as in Warsaw, but it seems both muggier and smoggier than the Polish capital. There's also more activity and hustle and bustle than in Warsaw Centralna – whole families are getting off the train with luggage for five people, bags of food and souvenirs – to be welcomed by family members who have wisely brought trolley carts and sack barrows along; backpackers with large blue-and-red backpacks are hesitantly making their way towards the end of the platform and the exit, and in between elderly men in crumpled suits offer taxi services in a variety of languages written on dirty pieces of cardboard. I say goodbye to the Szamborskis, who are being picked up by their friends, and wish them a nice holiday, while they wish me luck for my trip. I shoulder my bag and march off towards the exit. Stepping out of the station, I stop for a moment and attempt to properly take in my arrival on Russian soil: the noise of the cars beeping past, the wet smell emitting from the freshly scrubbed pavement drying in the sun, and the low-hanging tram cables over the street ... but to the sound of a variety of curses that I don't understand I'm immediately pushed aside by the flow of people leaving and entering the station.

6 INTERMISSION: *MOSKAU IST EIN SCHÖNES LAND*

Moscow and control of the camps

Moscow's a crazed old skull
of letter-eyed buildings,
a slave who hangs from a sword,
a slave of unwept evenings.

Velimir Khlebnikov, 'Moscow's A Crazed Old Skull'

I follow the signs to the metro, and it is surprisingly easy to buy a single ticket from the multilingual vending machine at the entrance. I'm not yet ready to face the expressionless members of proto-socialist Russian customer service that I imagine lurking behind every corner. I have studied the way to my rented apartment on Zubovsky Boulevard, near Park Kultury metro station, so I find my way to the right train easily and enjoy the fact that the Moscow metro is air-conditioned and has the most spacious subway trains I've ever seen. No comparison with the cramped London Tube – Moscow metro carriages feel like proper train carriages. After a few stops, I emerge in the afternoon heat and face ten lanes of boulevard traffic. According to my map, I just have to walk up the street, but suddenly I feel exhausted, my bag is getting heavier and heavier and the smog seems to increase with every step. And there are no proper traffic lights anywhere. I trot up the boulevard, past builders renovating the facade of a building with whining power drills, babushkas selling grapes and cherries from little plastic tables on the pavement, and men in business suits shouting angrily into their mobile phones. The street is end-less, and all buildings are massive and dwarf the pedestrians walking past – there seem to be no proper apartment buildings in sight, just huge grey office blocks and administrative build-ings 50, 60, 100 m long and another 60 m tall, the ground floors rented out to coffee shops, restaurants and electronic media stores. Large advertising boards scream down HTC! and Hyundai! at the tiny people walking past and the sweating Ger-man idiot. The constant rumble of the traffic just adds to my misery. I contemplate crossing the street and braving the traf-fic, but I have watched all those dash cam videos on YouTube and know that I would not make it across alive. After what feels like two more kilometres I finally find a pedestrian crossing that allows me to cross the street to where my apartment is lo-cated. The location is quite pleasant: a grey U of not overtly dominating apartment blocks with a small park in the middle that somewhat filters the traffic noise. I sit my bag down and take a deep breath. I have arrived in Moscow.

~

Cilly is still on the train. Two weeks now, and the guards have put on fur caps and thick coats. Sometimes, the trains stops for days on end, the guards knocking on carriage doors, walls and wheel axles, to find out if the prisoners have loosened planks to try to escape. The lice infestation has worsened. The cramped carriages are filled with itching and swearing women, trying to delouse each other in the twilight. At some stops, the women are again ordered from the trains and brought to a bathhouse. They are lucky: on most other trains leaving from occupied Germany, the women had to live with the dirt and the lice for the whole trip.

~

That the Russians could come any day was a known fact in West Germany when I grew up during the 1980s. Every month or so, the city would test the air-raid sirens, sending wailing howls out over the rooftops of Solingen and me crying into the arms of my mother. I remember being very afraid of something monstrous coming through the air towards me. I don't remember asking Cilly about the air-raid sirens because she told me before that there were no air-raid sirens in her village during the war, but I might have asked her about the Russians. And now I'm here, in the former centre of the evil Reds, bringing not only my prejudices and stereotypes, but also my baggage of Cold War memories with me. It will be hard to leave all this behind, but Moscow seems to be a good place to store it for a while. I'm sitting in a pompous Soviet train station, Kievskiy, which is adorned with red stars, flags and the face of Vladimir Lenin, and having a bout of xenophobia. I walked over here with no real purpose, just because it is around the corner from my apartment. But when I had to walk through a metal detector and past militiamen with machine guns just to enter the place, I freaked out a little and needed to sit down on a bench next to a kiosk selling mobile phones and sweets. I don't speak the language, my visa isn't registered yet, militia are everywhere and most of the locals look neither very friendly nor trustworthy. Perhaps it is all in my mind. I try to remember if I reacted the same way when I arrived in Poland three weeks ago. I assume so, but I still feel alone. I push myself up and decide to visit a church. Faith was important to Cilly, so maybe there's another clue to be found there.

At dusk, I reach the Cathedral of Christ the Saviour. It is a large and beautiful church on the northern bank of the River Moskva, a few blocks south-west of the Kremlin. At 103 m, it is the tallest Orthodox Christian church in the world, and it was once a swimming pool. The current church is the second to stand on this site, as the original was destroyed in 1931 under the orders of Stalin. It is massive and white and crowned

11 Cathedral of Christ the Saviour, Moscow

by five bulbous golden domes. The site, close to the Kremlin, was chosen by Czar Alexander I in 1837, but the cathedral took many decades to build and was finally consecrated in 1883.

I decide against going inside and just walk around the square surrounding the cathedral and then over towards the bridge that leads away from the square over the River Moskva. Here, long-legged Russian women in short skirts are posing for their boyfriends and husbands and lovers, leaning against the bridge's railings and throwing their hair back while being photographed and filmed. Groups of tourists wander past, some like me stopping mid-bridge to lean back and take in the impressive view of the city.

After the Revolution, and more specifically after the death of Lenin, the cathedral was chosen by Stalin as the perfect site for his giant monument to socialism, the Palace of the Soviets. This monument was to rise in buttressed tiers to support a gigantic statue of Lenin perched on top of a dome with his arm raised in the air in salute. I can understand why he'd want to be up there. From his position atop the socialist juggernaut, Lenin could have taken it all in at dusk, just as I am doing now: the red towers, white palace buildings and golden domes of the Kremlin glistening in the setting sun, the beeping evening commuter traffic along the banks of the Moskva and the tourist ships making their way down river; the large grey House on the Embankment apartment block on the other side of the river, where, during the Great Terror of the 1930s, the Soviet elite and intelligentsia lived and waited for the NKVD to knock on their door. On the other side of the bridge is the large former factory of 'Red October', which used to produce socialist chocolate and now houses bars and clubs and exhibition spaces. There is a monstrous statue of Czar Peter the Great standing on the bridge of a ship erected right in the water, towering over the factory building. The statue is allegedly based on a design originally intended to commemorate the 500th anniversary of the first voyage of Christopher Columbus, in 1992. When an American customer for the project could not be found, it was repurposed with a Russian theme. Despite all its crassness there is a certain beauty to Moscow, I realise then, and also that I am hungry. I walk towards the Red October area. My guidebook tells me I'll find pizza there.

The next day, I combine my visit to another location connected with Cilly's fate with a visit to the ultimate Moscow tourist destination: Red Square.

From the outside, the Kremlin isn't that impressive. It just looks like a big red castle and again, the only extraordinary feature is the enormous distance one covers to get from one end of the square to the other. I buy a water bottle from one of the street vendors and set off along the west wall, past the Trinity Gate Tower and the Tomb of the Unknown Soldier where, strangely, Russian couples like having their picture taken in front of the solemn guards and the burning eternal flame. Walking up the little hill past the equally red State History Mu-

seum and Kremlin Palace with its gold-cross-topped domes
and spires, I join the throng of tourists on Red Square only to
find that large parts of it are blocked off from visitors, seemingly for some kind of official festivity. The Lenin Mausoleum
is accessible, but after standing in the midday heat for a moment I decide that the mummy is not worth a lengthy wait. I
trudge across the square and into the grey hulk of the GUM,
the *Glavnyi Universalnyi Magazin*: main universal store. This
impressive nineteenth-century warehouse was commissioned
by Catherine II of Russia and nationalised after the 1917 Revolution. At the end of the Soviet era, GUM was privatised, and
had a number of owners before being sold to a supermarket
company. As a shopping mall, it was renamed in such a way
that it could still be called GUM. However, the first word
Gosudarstvennyi (state) has been replaced with *Glavnyi*
(main). Today, there is little difference between it and other
large luxury malls in Europe. There are hostesses in high heels
and short skirts in front of sports cars, there's the ubiquitous
Swarovski store, one perfumery after another and jewellery ga-
lore. I'm glad that the building is air-conditioned, and I use it
as a shortcut towards the north side of the square and the almost Disneyland-ish sight of St Basil's Cathedral which, with
its many colourful onion-domed spires, has become an iconic
image of Russia, perhaps even more so than Red Square itself.

St Basil's marks the geometric centre of Moscow and was
the city's tallest building until 1600, supposedly shaped like a
bonfire rising into the sky. As part of a programme of official
atheism, the church was confiscated by the Soviet state in 1924
and became part of the State Historical Museum in 1928. It was
completely and forcefully secularised in 1929 and remains the
property of the Russian Federation. I do not go inside, as it's
already swarming with other tourists. Instead, I look out over
Red Square and take a sip from my water bottle, thinking that
Cilly would have liked the church and its history, though not
it being secularised.

The sun is still beating down, and I finally decide to do one of the things I am in Moscow for. I cross the square again, this time leaving past Kazan Cathedral and walking through the gate of the Kremlin Palace. And there he is: right past the gate, standing next to a man dressed as Vladimir Ilyich Lenin, the man who brought my grandmother to the camps. Or somebody dressed up as him, in a light-brown marshal's uniform, smoking a pipe with a curved stem and stroking a moustache very similar to that of Joseph Vissarionovich Stalin. Families and children with ice cream and balloons walk past, and smiling Japanese tourists have their pictures taken with him. I wonder if any of them know of the files of the Polish officers to be shot at Katyn forest signed by this man, or what they would say to an actor dressed as Hitler standing at the Brandenburg Gate. Today I'm not here to pick a bone with Uncle Joe though; I'm here to see something else.

I walk past the hotels and theatres on Teatral'nyy Proyezd Boulevard, and soon stand amidst the fuming Moscow city traffic on the side of Lubyanka Square. Opposite is a square-cut beige building, the workplace of the men responsible for herding my grandmother and the other women into trains. The men might be dead by now, but their building survives: *Lubyanka.*

Designed by Alexander V Ivanov in 1897, Lubyanka was originally built in 1898 as the headquarters of the All-Russia Insurance Company. After 1917, the building was used as the headquarters of the secret police, the Cheka. Soon, the first political prisoners were brought here before being sentenced and exiled to Siberia. Muscovites began calling Lubyanka the 'tallest building in Moscow', since Siberia could be seen from its basement. Although the Soviet secret police changed its name many times, from NKVD to MVD and KGB, its headquarters remained the same. Secret police chiefs – from Lavrenty Beria to Yuri Andropov – used the same office on the third floor, which looked down on the statue of Cheka founder Felix Dzerzhinsky. A cell on the ground floor of the building features prominently in Aleksandr Solschenizyn's *The Gulag Archipelago*. Famous and infamous inmates from all over the world were tortured and interrogated here, real or imagined enemies of the Soviet Union: Jewish rescuer Raoul Wallenberg, former Romanian prime minister Ion Antonescu, Czech politician János Esterházy, the Jesuit Walter Ciszek and many, many more. After the dissolution of the KGB, the Lubyanka became the headquarters of the Federal Security Service of the Russian Federation, and today houses the Lubyanka prison and the Russian secret service: the Federal Security Service of the Russian Federation (FSB). There is also now a KGB museum. Cilly never saw the building, and she never knew of the men inside who decided her fate in the Soviet Union.

As Cilly was part of the 'interned and mobilised Germans', as the civil prisoners were called in the official language of Soviet authorities, she was considered a prisoner of war, not a political one. So it was not the official and infamous Gulag administration overseeing the 'archipelago' of camps immortalised by Solschenizyn, but another division of the Soviet secret service called Gupvi, the Main Administration for Affairs of Prisoners of War and Internees, that was responsible for the capture, transport and internment of the women.

First established within the NKVD in September 1939 following the Soviet invasion of Poland, the Gupvi established a system similar to the Gulag administration. Its major function was to organise foreign forced labour throughout the Soviet Union, both for official Wehrmacht and other Axis POWs as well as civilian prisoners. Whereas Gulag camps contained both political prisoners and convicted criminals, the Gupvi camps were mostly organised by nationality. The first Gupvi camps were constructed following Gulag camp plans, and conditions in both camp systems were similar: hard labour, poor nutrition and living conditions, high mortality rates during and in the first years after the war. The Soviet authorities used the Gupvi camps to recruit future Communist activists to send back to East Germany and the Polish People's Republic. To improve these recruitment initiatives, in the late 1940s and early 50s the camps also had clubs, libraries, stage shows and radio stations. During the existence of Gupvi from 1939 to 1953, there were over 500 POW camps in the Soviet Union and other Warsaw Pact states, which imprisoned over 4 million former soldiers and captured civilians.

Near where I stand is a monument to all those poor souls who entered the Gulag and Gupvi camps and did not make it out alive: a piece of rock. The Solovetsky Stone memorial was erected in 1990 outside the building that housed the architects of captivity to commemorate the victims of political repression, and I'll pause here for a moment after staring at Lubyanka for a while. The stone is a grey-brown slab of granite, sitting askew on a platform of polished granite, inscribed on the four sides with the words 'To prisoners of Gulag', 'To victims of Communist Terror', 'To Freedom Fighters' and a line from Anna Akhmatova's poem *Requiem*: 'I wish to call all of them by name, but...'

Compared with Red Square, which was heaving with people, the small square here with the stone at its centre is deserted. To my left there's a metro entrance, to my right the intimidating, watchful presence of Lubyanka, and behind me, under the trees on the square, a few drunks are asleep on park benches in the shade. The whole square is encircled by parked cars. But I still feel that the stone has found its rightful place. Significantly, it replaced the mighty statue of Dzerzhinsky, the founder of the Cheka, that once stood here. And the stone has come a long way, from the Solovetsky Islands in the White Sea, where the first Gulag camp was formed in 1927.

I sit down on a bench, take a sip from my water bottle and think that the unobtrusive stone is a fitting memorial, a symbol without pomp for all those innocent and random victims shovelled into the mouth of war and terror just because they said something wrong to a colleague, or refused to flee their home when the soldiers arrived. I am also angry, angry at men long dead. At the imbecile Führer and the other moustachioed megalomaniac with the pipe; but more specifically at little bastard minions like the East Prussian Gauleiter Erich Koch. He, like all good mid-level minions, kept the people under his control in place until they could no longer run from the Red Army – and then, like the coward he was, declared he would fight to the end at Königsberg, only to escape in his private boat to Denmark. At Laverenti Beria, who ran the NKVD when Cilly was taken. He used to club people around the stomach with a piece of rubber hose until their guts came wriggling out; he sent the women he raped to the Gulag so they could not tell on him. Power-drunk men who facilitated evil, agents of darkness. I push myself up and walk back to the metro and my apartment. They sell cheap Czech beer at the kiosk nearby.

The next day, I visit the Gulag museum, another item on my Moscow list. The State Museum of Gulag History was founded in 2001, and its first exhibition opened in 2004. The museum's founder, Anton Antonov-Ovseenko, a historian and writer, was a prisoner of Stalin's labour camps. The museum holds permanent and travelling exhibitions of its own collections and works in collaboration with other museums and archives, private collectors, painters and photographers. It also hosts conferences, concerts, theatre performances, readings and other events.

It is hard to find. From Pushkinskaya metro station, I first walk in the wrong direction down Tverskoy Boulevard past tourist groups and begging babushkas, until I realise my mistake and walk back up Strastnoy Boulevard. I finally crisscross a maze of streets lined with colourful nineteenth-century merchant houses, decrepit Orthodox churches and crumbling Communist building blocks, until I find a small sign at the entrance to a courtyard on Petrovka Street, right opposite the Marriott hotel.

The barbed wire and watchtower erected in the cramped courtyard stand in stark contrast to the restaurants and upscale boutiques lining the street. I had expected a brighter and more modern place, but the building, which is an average Moscow apartment building, has seen better days. Black-and-white photographs of political prisoners who died in the Gulag hang in the courtyard, pictures of priests, soldiers, clerks, theatre directors. The museum entrance is a small metal door, and the clerk selling tickets does not speak English. The exhibition is dedicated to the history of the development, rise and decline of the Soviet labour camp system, an instrumental and integral part of the Soviet state from the 1930s to the 1960s. The exhibition also serves as a home for the stories of various people who were victims of repressive Soviet policy and sentenced to serve in labour camps. One room is dedicated to the Soviet policy of falsifying official photographs, removing or blacking out members of the government who had subsequently been sent to a Gulag.

In the basement, I find a reconstruction of a prisoner's barrack. It is dark, maybe 3 m wide and 4 m long, the walls crude planks, lined with bunk beds on both sides, and a small stove and table in the middle of the room. The 'beds' are just wooden planks on wooden bed frames; no blankets, no nothing. For the first time I see in real life what Cilly's bed of four years looked like. I touch the planks and try to imagine sleeping on hard wood for such a long time, and what it would do to my back. There are other visitors around, so I don't feel like I can sneak onto it for a moment. It does not look comfortable. A large map of the Soviet Union shows the vast network of camps across the countries, where men and women of countless nationalities slaved away for the glory of Stalinism. As I leave, the sun is setting.

At the time of my visit the museum occupied just 300 of the 3,000 square metres of the building it was originally planned for, and fewer than 3,000 people visited the city-funded museum between 2005 and 2006, the only years for which data are available. In 2015 however, the authorities opened a new, spacious museum dedicated to the millions who were persecuted in the Gulag system. Like its hidden predecessor, the new five-storey museum in the Meshchansky district north of Moscow city centre shows personal effects of Gulag prisoners, the dimensions of prison cells, and original doors from camps in remote Magadan, Anadyr and Vorkuta.

The next day, I discover that Moscow is not all hectic and new money and giant slabs of concrete which block a view of the past. In the evening I'm standing opposite the arched entrance to Gorky Park, waiting for Moscow journalists Elenka Bobrova and Sasha Guzeva, who have agreed to give me a tour of Muzeon Park just across the street.

Muzeon Park is located in front of the concrete hulk of the Krymsky Val building, which houses the Tretyakov Gallery of modern art and the Central House of Artists. Next to the entrance is a large bronze statue of workers, peasant women and a soldier wielding a machine gun; from there, gravel paths snake across green lawns strewn with statues. Gazing into the park while waiting for Elenka and Sasha, I had a slight James Bond feeling seeing all the old Communist statues standing around. The park was established by the City of Moscow in 1992 and displays over 700 sculptures, statues and monuments, including many old Communist statues. But this is not a scene from the *GoldenEye* movie with thugs lurking behind crumbling Lenin statues; this is a pleasant and quiet place.

'You won't find any henchmen lurking around here!' Sasha laughs. She and Elenka are two friendly Muscovites in summer dresses whom I met online while researching, and their newspaper interviewed me before I set off to Russia. They asked if I wanted to meet up to chat about my grandmother, trains and Gulags once I had arrived, and suggested Muzeon Park to meet.

'The park is even split into themed sections: there is the

Oriental Garden, the Pushkin Square, the Portrait Row and so on,' Elenka says.

'The fallen Soviet monuments appeared here shortly after the fall of Communism in 1991. When the Soviet Union collapsed, the more portable statues of Soviet leaders, workers and peasants were removed from their pedestals, hauled to the park and just left here.'

We walk down gravel paths past a few brown Stalins with missing noses, a white Lenin with weeds sprouting around his feet and a grey Brezhnev without legs, and reach the large bronze statue of Dzerzhinsky, the one that used to stand in front of Lubyanka. The tall man with the cape and the musketeer moustache and goatee still looks slightly menacing – but also somewhat lost, as if he is no longer taken seriously.

'After the city administration declared the area an official park in 1992, walkways were added along with small ponds, a snack bar and further statues from all over the former Soviet Union. This is why there are so many Stalins and Lenins,' Sasha says.

She also tells me that she wrote her thesis about the Gulag system and the camps, and I think this is a good thing, a sign that Russian society is willing to deal with the past. They're putting Communist statues up again, but only in the context of a small park near the water, not in public squares.

We come to another memorial, and when Sasha explains the history of this one I feel a glow of hope.

'In 1998, the park acquired this piece, made of small sculptures representing the victims of the Communist rule and the terror of the '30s, made by artist Evgeny Chubarov.'

Sasha is pointing at a large wall of faces: hundreds of heads sculpted from different stones, blue men with full beards, small black women with haggard faces and eyes closed, chubby and bald brown men, grey babushkas with their features almost completely erased, all confined behind a screen of rusting metal bars and barbed wire. It is a simple piece of art and I easily understand the intention of Chubarov: he is showing us the faces of our colleagues, friends and family.

'And look there,' Elenka says. 'There is the man from Lubyanka again!'

There is another statue of Dzerzhinsky, this one capturing him mid-stride wearing a suit and carrying a manila folder in one hand, like all the other mass murderers of the twentieth century.

Elenka and Sasha take me to Gorky Park next, 'where all Muscovites go in summer'. The Gorky Central Park of Culture and Leisure, as it is officially called, has always spurred my imagination, thanks to Martin Cruz Smith's novel named after the park and a line in 'Wind of Change' by Scorpions, the self-proclaimed soundtrack to the fall of Communism performed by four ageing German rockers from Hannover. To me, Gorky Park always seemed something prototypically Soviet.

It opened in 1928 and is located just across the River Moskva from Park Kultury metro station and opposite Muzeon Park. It was created by combining the public grounds of the

12 *Gulag memorial by Evgeny Chubarov*

old Golitsyn Hospital and the Neskuchny Palace gardens, and covers an area of 300 acres along the river. During the early post-Soviet era, Gorky Park used to host an amusement park with funfairs, amusement rides and even a Ferris wheel.

'Over the years, the rides became decrepit, and the park was swamped with cheap attractions and cafes,' Sasha explains.

'In 2011, Gorky Park underwent a major reconstruction. The city abolished the entrance fee and cleared the park of outdated carnival rides and junk food stalls, while at the same time bringing back more sport activities: aerobics, yoga, salsa dancing and so on.'

I am surprised by how orderly it is. There are thousands of people in the park and many children, all rollerblading, jogging or lying on sun loungers, some drinking beer from cans or eating ice cream. But it's not noisy or hectic. It feels like the Moscow that I experienced during the last few days is waiting outside the gate, denied entrance. There are ping-pong tables set out for free use as well, but not just two or three like in German parks, but 30 or 40 in a row, with Muscovites of all ages playing without any swearing or shouting. Fairy lights are hanging in the branches and I see the tail fin of what looks like an aeroplane behind some trees, glistening in the setting sun as we continue on to the Moskva. As I point this out to Elenka she laughs·

'This is no airplane, but a spaceship! It's one of the test units of the Soviet space shuttle programme, a shuttle called Buran. But it never flew, so in the end they put it here.'

Then we come to another strange sight. Along the banks of the river are a series of interlinked concrete platforms, some sort of esplanade. Each platform is occupied by groups of dancers: there is a group doing classical nineteenth-century ball dances, some of the women wearing long white ball gowns; another group is performing what looks like a line dance (no cowboy hats though), and the next platform is filled with waltzing couples. Michael Jackson's 'Man in the Mirror' is blaring from loudspeakers all along the esplanade, and I wonder how the dancers are able to fit all their different dance steps to a pop beat from the '80s. The sun has set as we climb up the stairs to the Pushkinsky Pedestrian Bridge, which connects the park with the Khamovniki district on the other side of the river. As we look down on the dancers and rollerbladers and fairy lights and street lights in the park and their reflections glittering on the river, Elenka asks: 'Moscow is a lot like Berlin, don't you think?'

I accompany Sasha and Elenka to what they call a 'youth centre' across the river. I imagine one of the small communal centres they have in Germany, with run-down cafes and crèches, but we end up in a beer garden in front of a colossal concrete building from Soviet times with cinemas, gaming arcades and two restaurants. I marvel at the Communist energy for building and approach to size over two beers and then we head off. As we say goodbye near the metro station, I ask how they'll get home.

'Oh, we'll just stop a car,' Sasha says.

'A taxi, you mean.'

She laughs. 'No, a car. You can just wave down cars on the road and if the driver is going your way he might take you for a tiny contribution towards the cost of fuel. It's cheaper than a taxi.'

Try that in Berlin, I think, and you would be declared a madman. But I like the Russian approach to life and its challenges: we'll get there in the end, don't worry.

The next morning, I'm sitting in the ticket hall of Kursky, one of the main train stations connecting Moscow to the East. As usual, I'm sweating. The main hall is underground, tiled in green with ticket desks in front of me, and to my right is the gate to the platforms, guarded by a stout-looking Russian woman in uniform. Whether or not I'm at the right gate, I couldn't say. Again, not being able to read Cyrillic has thwarted me. It took me a while to get here as I got lost in the endless corridors leading away from the metro station and spent an age going up and down lifts and staircases, until I finally emerged here in this large hall where noisy groups of travellers queue at ticket desks, try to extract chocolate bars from vending machines or have loud discussions with the uniformed guards protecting the entrance to the platforms. I have an hour to spare before the departure of my train to Yekaterinburg, so I sit down on my bag and ponder my stay in the Russian capital.

Moscow is a strange city. It is a place where every way is a long way and everything is intermingled: babushkas sell fruit and vegetables right next to a smoggy ten-lane street while businessmen park their American sports cars in front of dilapidated 24-hour shops, and tourists run around in confusion, hoping to find another museum, the only fixed points in this monumental concrete habitat of cars and brutalist architecture. The city has a queer sense of being incomplete, despite all the wealth that is presently amassed here. A city of marble-adorned metro stations full of beggars and sweaty street kids in tracksuit bottoms. It's too much, too big and too confusing. I always thought of myself as an experienced traveller, somebody who easily understands structures. In situations where other, less experienced travellers might spend hours identifying the layout of an airport, I would just zip past, with a smile. But in Moscow, I'm little short of a nervous wreck, suffering pangs of xenophobia I last encountered when I was 15 and knew nothing of the world, and several times I'm on the brink of aborting my journey and boarding the next plane back to Berlin. I'm just an effete product of my age and society, boisterous when it comes to staring at a screen and typing things onto an empty page, but when I really need to take the next step and leave my comfort zone, I hesitate and nervously send another email from the safety of my air-conditioned hotel room, instead of asking the next person on the street for help, in the fear they might not understand me. Travel writer my ass.

Moscow almost defeated me, and now I'm sitting here, only 20 minutes before my train departs to take me even further away from the safe boundaries of my life and into the unknown. I stand up, gather my belongings and approach the turnstiles. I show the guard my ticket and point towards the platforms. She thoroughly reviews my ticket, laughs, shakes her head and points to another flight of stairs at the end of the hall. I am wrong again.

I make it to the main platform hall, a large line of platforms covered by a metal roof, and find my train (going to Krasnoyarsk, Красноярск – see, it is not that hard) just in time. My carriage is guarded by two *provodnitsas* with perms and armed with clipboards, who only need a moment to double-check my passport number against the number on their list before ushering me on board. During my last minutes in town, Moscow is surprisingly obliging towards me. I step onto the train and don't look back.

～

The doors of the wagon clatter open, and the winter sun shines into the car. Cilly and Angelika blink into the bright square of the open door and a grey wall behind it. A guard cries '*Dawai! Dawai!*' again, but the women take their time. This will be another stop for a roll call or a bath, so why the hurry? They are weak, and roll groaningly to their side and then slowly rise to their feet. There's space now in the wagon. A quarter of the women who boarded in Insterburg four weeks ago are dead. The guards wave at them with their guns, and the women climb from the train with creaking joints, as slow as the extremely elderly. In front of them is the grey wall of a train station, with a decrepit platform and crumbling wooden station building. Behind the building, dark smoke is rising from hundreds of factory chimneys into the grey sky. They have arrived.

7 HUNGER

I think we are in rats' alley
Where the dead men lost their bones.

T.S. Eliot, The Waste Land

My grandmother was always feeding me. On an average Saturday, when my parents dropped me off at her house in the morning, the menu went as follows: for breakfast, there was porridge with cocoa and extra sugar and rolls with butter and thick slices of stinky old gouda; lunch was fatty meatballs with mash and gravy followed by vanilla ice cream smothered in hot cherry sauce, and when I settled on the sofa under a blanket after that there were crisps and chocolate bars and a glass of milk to wash it all down.

An hour or two later, when I was still unable to move because of my swollen belly, there was coffee and cake: thick slices of cheesecake or marble cake drowning in cream, and hot coffee with cream served in gold-rimmed cups. And an hour after coffee came dinner: breaded chicken cutlets fried in butter with cucumber salad and rye bread with more butter and malt beer. By the time my parents picked me up again in the evening I was delirious.

One of my two favourite dishes was her chicken soup, a whole boned and jointed chicken (with innards, which I didn't like) cooked with carrots and onions and served with potatoes and rice. My grandfather used to fish the heart out of the soup pot as a special treat – he liked innards. The other was *Königsberger Klopse*. These are meatballs in a creamy white sauce with capers, usually served with boiled potatoes and a bowl of apple sauce on the side. The dish is named after the Prussian capital city of Königsberg and remains one of the highlights of East Prussian and classic German cuisine. In the GDR, officials renamed the dish *Kochklopse* (boiled meatballs) to avoid any reference to its namesake, which had been annexed by the Soviet Union. The city's German inhabitants had been expelled, and the city renamed after a close ally of Stalin in the Soviet leadership, Mikhail Kalinin, becoming Kaliningrad. The GDR forbade using the historic names of annexed territories or cities.

Cilly heaped all that food on me because she didn't want me to be hungry. Not for a second, not ever.

KÖNIGSBERGER KLOPSE

Preparation time 30 minutes, total time 1 hour 15 minutes. Serves 4.

Ingredients:

For the meatballs:

  1 day old bread roll
  ⅛ litre lukewarm milk
  500 g veal mince
  1 large egg
  2–4 anchovies, finely chopped
  2 onions, finely chopped
  1 teaspoon butter
  3 tablespoons chopped parsley
  Zest of 1 small organic lemon
  400 ml beef or veal stock
  Freshly cracked black pepper

For the sauce:

    30 g butter
    25 g flour
    3 tablespoons capers
    2 tablespoons lemon juice
    125 ml cream
    125 ml dry white wine
    A pinch of sugar
    Freshly cracked black pepper
    2 egg yolks
    Salt

To make the meatballs, tear the bread roll into pieces and soak in the milk until soft. Mix together with the ground veal and egg. Add most of the chopped parsley and the lemon zest. Melt the butter in a large pan and sweat the onions until fragrant and transparent. Add to the ground veal together with the finely chopped anchovies. Mix well and form approximately 16 meatballs. Bring the stock to a boil, and then reduce to a gentle simmer. Add the meatballs and cook them for about ten minutes. Remove and set the meatballs aside, then strain the stock and reserve for the sauce.

To make the sauce, melt 30 g butter in a large pot. Sprinkle with the flour and cook until golden. Pour in the stock a bit at a time and whisk until the mixture is smooth. Add the capers, lemon juice, cream and wine. Season with salt, sugar and pepper.

Lightly beat the egg yolks and whisk into the sauce, making sure it does not boil. Slowly add the meatballs to the sauce and allow them to heat through. Serve with the rest of the parsley, lemon wedges and steamed or boiled potatoes.

~

The hunger is like toothache in Cilly's stomach. She would have never thought it, but hunger hurts. It's pulsating like the pain in a chipped tooth. The room is dark and she is supposed to sleep, but her thoughts keep circling around her empty stomach and the journey. She was not as hungry during the first days of her journey on account of the rations she had packed. The cheese and ham had been a welcome addition to the meagre provisions their captors had dished out. So until the camp in Insterburg, the hunger had not been more than a nuisance, something she might feel after a long day hiking. But after a day on the train she ran out of food, and she and the others had to make do with the hard bread the Russians threw into the carriage.

She's lying on top of a wooden bunk bed, Angelika next to her. There are two more women lying on the bunk below. There are 19 more bunks around them, in two rows of ten, all filled with female prisoners, most of them sleeping. In the middle of the room is a small stove that is supposed to warm their barracks, but Cilly's bed is close to the door where it is cold. The barracks are made from wooden planks, the walls are unplastered, the cracks in the planks stopped with mud. The floor is dried mud too. The roof is built at a sharp angle, but low to the ground. It reeks of unwashed humans and cheap coal and decay.

The dirty and torn clothes Angelika and Cilly had been wearing have been replaced with some grey uniform pieces they were given when they reached the camp; both use a dirty overcoat as a blanket. The Wehrmacht insignia on the sleeves of the tunic and coat had been removed, but Cilly recognised it anyway as formerly belonging to a German soldier. She does not wonder about its former owner. There are no pillows, and they use a piece of plank to prop up their heads. From the train, they had marched past dirty concrete buildings, long rows of wooden shacks and tall chimneys which belched out smoke into the winter sky; everything was brown-grey, and barbed wire sealed them off from the outside world. The wide plains of Russia were nowhere to be seen. Instead, Cilly thinks of pictures she has seen of the industrial towns near the Ruhr in Germany, where the Krupp armament company built their canons. She asked one of the guards where they were, and he said: 'Nizhny Tagil.'

Nizhny Tagil, today a city in Sverdlovsk Oblast in Russia, lies 25 kilometres east of the border between Europe and Asia. It is an industrial town with a large portion of the cityscape dominated by factories. It also has the dubious honour of being the Russian city with the largest number of prisons.

The city was founded in 1722. Over the following decades, it developed into one of the early centres of Russian industrialisation, and it has been a major producer of cast iron and steel ever since. But the real transformation of 'Tagil', as its inhabitants call it, began with the German invasion in 1941. Refugees and workers ordered here increased the population in the first months of the war from 150,000 to 500,000, and about 40 complete factories and industrial institutions were evacuated here from the west, away from the German invaders. In December 1941, just a couple of weeks after the new workers arrived, the city was already able to send the first trainloads of T-34 tanks to the front lines. Not only did the people of the city work in the factories, there was also a lot of construction work, most of it done by Russian Gulag prisoners. They built great parts of the Nizhny Tagil Iron and Steel Plant, the coke plant, the metalworking plants, the car repair factory and much more.

Later, the Russian Gulag inmates were replaced by POWs from the Axis nations moving into Gupvi camps. The first POW camp in Nizhny Tagil was built in 1943 for German and Hungarian prisoners, with many of the German, Hungarian and Romanian survivors of the Battle of Stalingrad transported here. It was a huge camp consisting of one central and 12 sub-camps, the so-called *lagpunkts*. These smaller camps were dedicated to a variety of purposes and products: there was a wagon factory, camps for roadworks and construction, earthworks, ammunition and weapon factories, a quarry, forest camps, a camp farm, and an opencast pit for iron ore mining. Prisoners were kept in wooden and clay barracks and some even in crude earth bunkers dug into the ground. Temperatures were merciless: endless winters came with snowstorms and temperatures of minus 30 degrees Celsius, whereas summers scorched and temperatures surpassed 38 degrees Celsius, with dust and midges filling the polluted air.

Thousands of prisoners of war passed through Nizhny Tagil, and for many it was the last place they would see on earth. When Cilly arrived in March 1945, there was a cemetery with over 4,000 graves near military hospital number 2929 (mostly dug by German prisoners for their deceased comrades), and the Russians had recently ordered a mass grave to be dug. Between October 1944 and March 1945, about 1,000 people died here, from dysentery, dystrophy, typhus, pneumonia and frostbite. Most were women.

Lagpunkt 7153 was Cilly's camp, an all-female compound. After disembarking from the train there was a roll call and the women were sorted into rows of five, with NKVD guards writing their names on large clipboards, then they were herded to the camp, about 30 minutes' march from the station. At the camp, Cilly and the other women were issued with their uniforms. These were either old Wehrmacht uniforms or the standard clothing issued for Soviet labour camps: a black tunic, quilted pants, a long quilted outer jacket, a felt hat with ear flaps, rubber-soled boots and fleece-lined mittens. The items and uniforms were handed out indiscriminately from a large shed by the guards, and it was up to the women to find the right sizes. Everything was either too small or too big, and the prisoners spent hours trading for a better fit. It was the only thing to do anyway – there was no food, and at nightfall they were all sent to their barracks.

In March 1945, the average temperature was between minus four and zero, and there was still a thick layer of snow and
frost on the ground. There were about 3,500 displaced people
and POWs living and working in the Nizhny Tagil camp, plus
an additional 1,800 women from East Prussia that included the
300 survivors from Cilly's transport. Of these 1,800 women,
1,200 would be dead within six months.

~

I am on the train again. Unlike my cabin from Warsaw, my
Russian one has four berths and a small table in the middle
directly under the window, decorated with a plastic tablecloth.
The berths are padded with red leather, there are green curtains on the windows, the walls are grey plastic and there is
even a cheap red plastic carpet. I'm in *kupe*, second class. All
carriages have four-berth compartments and nine compartments per carriage with washrooms and toilets at the end of
the corridor. I heave my bags onto the top left bunk, and sit
down with a Russian beer and some crisps as the train stutters
from the station. After a few minutes, my fellow passengers enter the compartment: a young student couple from the look of
it, both tall and skinny and blonde, the man in a polo shirt and
blue jeans, the woman wearing a tight black T-shirt and black
cotton trousers. After a brief nod, they store their bags under
the lower bunk on their side, then settle down with a tablet and
a small laptop, plug in headphones and watch films, so it
seems. They don't talk to each other.

I lean back and sip my beer while reading a book about the
Warsaw Uprising. I'm not sure if I can put down the feeling of
estrangement that I've been carrying around since Moscow to
the simple fact that I don't speak Russian. Having talked to a
few locals and after trying to navigate the country and the capital for a few days, it is easy to see that Russia functions like any

other first world country. Young workers live in shared apartments and houses and have to commute endlessly because everything in the city centre is too expensive. Every passenger on the metro reads some kind of tablet. And the *provodnitsas* just check your passport number the same way their German counterparts would, and don't immediately report you to the militia as a foreign spy. Many of my expectations were stereotypes and nothing else. Maybe my feeling of estrangement comes from the fact that the ideas and concepts of Russia I developed based on Cilly's stories don't survive my encounter with the real Russia.

After a while we stop, and most people clamber from the train. I abandon my fear of pickpockets and follow the other passengers. There are groups of vendors on the platform, men, women, children, and they offer a weird variety of goods: tea glasses, beer, teddy bears, fruit, cooked chicken and even plastic chandeliers. No vending machines or timetables or even rubbish bins are visible on the platform, just the strange vendors. So here travellers are supplied by humans, not by machines. On one side of the train there's a line of green-grey carriages, and on the other side another cracked platform with a few lonely trees behind it. Three hours from Moscow, I wonder where I am.

I find out as we roll into a city with a nice array of onion domes on a hill a few hours later. This is Yaroslavl, as my travel book confirms. Here we get a fourth travel companion, a tiny young brunette lady somewhere between 20 and 25, with a bright red shirt, blue jeans, false nails and a dressing over her left ear. After storing her bags under the lower bunk, she changes from trainers into slippers, like all the other passengers. I feel bad for not bringing any. I only have trainers. We introduce ourselves with a quick 'Hi' and settle back in our bunks, each on one side of the bunk on our side. A few moments after leaving Yaroslavl, we cross a wide river via a metal bridge, and the others become agitated, stepping out into the corridor and taking pictures of the river from the windows on both sides of the carriage. It's a wide river with forests on the left and right banks and a few sand bars in the middle, and it takes us almost five minutes to cross its gunmetal grey waters. I ask the couple what the name of the river is, already guessing their response: 'We just crossed the Volga!'

Now only Cilly has made it further east. Even my grandfather Willy, if he served with Army Group South, the part of the Wehrmacht that reached Stalingrad and the Caucasus, never crossed the Volga. Does that fact make me feel different? I don't know. I just lean back and continue listening to the clack-clack, clack-clack of the train wheels.

～

In the camp, in the morning just after sunrise there is another roll call, by now routine for the prisoners. Afterwards Cilly, Angelika and the others are directed by the guards to a small wooden shed, where two German women in padded coats hand out empty metal tins and wooden spoons to the new arrivals. Cilly does not recognise anyone except Angelika. All the other women from her transport have been moved to other barracks. Despite everything she has seen, she is shocked by how young the other women around her are – most are gaunt teenagers between 14 and 18, huddled together in shivering groups. 'Look at them!' one of the women snorts in German, a tall blonde with a large mole on her forehead who is handing out spoons. 'They won't make it long.' Cilly just stares at her until Angelika pulls her away and leads her in the direction of a larger shed with a smoking chimney.

'There will be no replacements!' the woman shouts after them. 'So don't lose your spoons, you bitches!'

The large shed is the kitchen and mess hall. A dark room filled with crude wooden tables and benches and the sound of spoons scraping tins. No one talks, everyone just stares into their own tin. Cilly and Angelika walk towards a small window in the wall, to another woman with a stained brown headscarf, who splashes two spoonfuls of a watery gruel into their tins, brown water with bits of buckwheat and cabbage leaves. She also hands them two slices of wet and sticky rye bread each.

'More bread tonight for dinner. Do you want tea?'

'Yes please,' Cilly says.

'Empty your tins and come back here after you finish eating. And whatever you do, don't lose your crockery. Otherwise you'll have to get others to lend you theirs – we are not allowed to hand out food to prisoners without receptacles.'

'Thank you. My name is Cilly – short for Cäcilie.'

'I'm Doris. I'm from the Banat. Where did they take you from?'

'Near Allenstein.'

'East Prussia, hmm? I heard they will be in Berlin soon and the war will end. Hopefully we can all go home then. Hurry up with the breakfast, they normally send newcomers to work straight away.'

'Thanks again, Doris.'

Cilly and Angelika sit down on an empty bench, and Cilly starts to wolf down the gruel until Angelika puts a hand on her arm.

'Slowly. I don't think there will be a second helping after that, so take your time. Maybe we can even save a piece of bread and eat it later.'

'But Angelika, I'm so hungry!'

'I know. But I don't know how long it will be like this.'

~

It would be long. It would be another year at least, another year of people starving to death, before Soviet authorities were willing and able to improve the prisoners' diet. The Soviet authorities did not starve them on purpose. The situation was the result of both a disastrous lack of supplies owing to four long years of devastating war, the fact that the Red Army in the field received supplies first, and an unbalanced distribution of the available supplies to the respective camps. That some camp commanders decided to withhold large parts of their supplies for their own purposes did not improve the situation of German POWs and civilian prisoners during the last months of the war in 1945 and the beginning of 1946. Nevertheless, the prisoners were expected to work.

For three weeks, I tried to emulate a similar diet to the one Cilly and her fellow prisoners had to endure for almost two years. It meant I had to learn hunger. My daily ration was 200 grams of rye bread and two helpings of *kasha*, buckwheat porridge, for breakfast and dinner. Lunch was a watery soup of potatoes, carrots and spinach (as a stand-in for the nettles the prisoners sometimes used), with only unsweetened black tea and water to drink. The first few days I felt good, losing my cravings for sugary food and alcohol after two or three days. Then, after receiving the same food for a week, I could feel my body change. I woke up starving, but instead of welcoming my morning bowl of buckwheat gruel, my stomach would sigh after the first spoonful, as again nothing nourishing was forthcoming. I started losing weight fast – after five days my body started to take the energy it needed from itself, burning surplus fat. I was constantly hungry, not as in having an appetite, but instead having the real and constant feeling that something was not right in my body. The hunger manifested itself in pain, a proverbial stomach like a clenched fist that was the focus of my thoughts every waking minute. I was actually looking forward to going to sleep, as it meant getting closer to my next meal in the morning, even if it was only boring buckwheat. In the end, I lost 10 kilograms in four weeks. Cilly was always talking about the 'poor girls from town who died like flies', and I can imagine the strain on the bodies of these young women, especially if they were not accustomed to physical labour, as

Cilly was from her work on the farm.

Dystrophy, and the most severe type of malnutrition catabolysis, the process of a body breaking down its own tissues to keep vital systems such as the nervous system and heart muscle functioning, is what kills the prisoners. As Stefan Karner points out in 'In the GUPVI Archipelago' (*Im Archipel GUPVI*):

> Dystrophy was the reason for more than half of the deaths occurring among Austrian and German prisoners, followed by infectious diseases like dysentery and typhus. The hunger dwarfs all other needs and leads to an extreme shift in values. For a piece of bread prisoners were willing to sacrifice everything else. During the medical examination of the POWs and the subsequent classification into work brigades, prisoners are determined as undernourished or not by the so-called 'indecent grab', the physical verification of enough meat and fat reserves in the buttocks.

Without roughly 120 grams of glucose a day, the human brain starts to malfunction. After two or three days without food, the body begins to burn the fat stored in the chest, abdomen and around the kidneys, but the central nervous system cannot survive on such fats. Instead, the brain uses ketone produced by the liver as it processes body fat. When the body's fat reserves are exhausted, the protein in the body becomes the brain's chief source of energy. In effect, a human brain begins to eat its body's muscles to survive. This is the moment when starvation begins. Symptoms include dry eyes, spongy bleeding gums, enamel mottling, loose and wrinkled skin, thin and soft nail plates, loss of knee and ankle reflexes, and poor memory.

For dinner on the train I have half a cooked chicken, rye bread, butter, crisps and another beer. But that is nothing compared with what my fellow passengers dish out: all brought at least four different Tupperware boxes filled with potato or noodle salads, pieces of cucumber, chicken fillet and meatballs.

They have cutlery and plastic plates, napkins and even wet wipes. I wipe my grease-stained fingers on the chicken wrappings and once again feel unprepared. Over dinner, we start to converse, in English. Yulia, the petite woman on my side of the cabin, is from Siberia and has an ear infection, which is why she has to take the train.

'I'm travelling from Yaroslavl to Novosibirsk, which means two days on the train. I'd prefer to fly, but...' she says, pointing at her bandaged left ear.

The student couple are Tatyana and Vadim, and they will share our compartment until Perm, where they'll visit Tatyana's parents.

'We'd prefer to fly as well,' Vadim says, 'and I guess the only advantage Russian trains have over flying is the cheapness of train tickets.'

To the young Russian, local train travel is not as exciting as it sounds. After all, they do it all the time. While tourists may recall their times on the Trans-Siberian railway with watery eyes, most Russians would prefer to fly.

As the sun sets, the scenery outside the window changes. After the concrete suburbs of Moscow and Yaroslavl and the factories around the cities, it is now forest for hours and hours. It starts to rain and gets dark fast, and we all start to prepare our beds. At least this drill I know from the Warsaw train. Yulia and I step out into the corridor to leave the students to prepare their bunks, then they step out and Yulia does the same, and finally it's the turn of the German idiot to fumble around with his bedding under the scrutinising eyes of the Russians. I walk to the washroom to brush my teeth, past the *provodnitsa* who stands in the corridor with a colleague smoking a cigarette. She grunts in my direction, which I hope is a good sign. The washroom is small, mostly stainless steel and surprisingly clean. There's even a short piece of plastic hose hanging from the water tap, and I've read that this can be used as an impromptu shower on longer train journeys. But I showered this morning in Moscow and will only spend one night on the train, so I wash my face and brush my teeth. I walk back to my compartment, where everyone else is already lying on their bunks. I bed down for the night, while the train continues its journey into the darkness of Russia.

~

After breakfast, there's another roll call and the prisoners are marched out of the gate and along a gravel road. The guards don't shout, and the prisoners are allowed to talk. Cilly whispers to a young woman walking beside her.

'I'm Cilly.'

The girl, who can't be older than 16, is tiny and wears her long brown hair in two dirty pigtails. She just stares at the ground and walks on mechanically.

'Do you know what day it is? It is my birthday in April, and I'm afraid I might have missed it.'

'They shot Mama,' the young woman whispers.

'Leave her, please,' an older woman walking behind the girl says to Cilly.

'She hasn't been herself since she was taken and had to witness her mother getting shot in Königsberg. She could not walk fast enough.'

Cilly nods.

'And it is the end of March, by the way. When is your birthday?'

'The 21st of April.'

'Ha, one day after the Führer!' the woman snorts. 'So you're lucky. You can thank him that we're in this mess.'

The prisoners are marched alongside train tracks lined with barbed wire. They're ordered to stop in front of a large shaft tower, two small brick buildings and heaps of crude chunks of black coal, partially covered in snow.

'*Dawai!* You'll need to empty the trolleys coming up from

the mine! Quick!'

A short man in prisoner clothing with a club in his hands has appeared from one of the buildings and points to a row of dented metal carts standing on tracks under the shaft tower. The tracks lead to a ramp from where the carts or trolleys can be emptied into an open freight car on one side or a large slag heap on the other. Three or four other women who speak Russian translate the foreman's words to their companions. Cilly is relieved. For a moment she was afraid they would be forced to work underground.

The women pull and push the creaking carts to the freight cars and tilt them, the coal tumbling down until the car is full and another is pushed into its place. When there's no freight car, they pour the coal onto the slag heap. The tracks from the shaft tower to the ramp are about 300 metres long, or 437 steps, as Cilly counts. The women moan and groan as they push the carts. Half of them are seamstresses, secretaries, teachers, and they have never done such work in their lives. There are bad and good trolleys. Some wheels don't move at all, so the trolleys have to be dragged rather than rolled; some derail easily; some are so dented they hardly fit into the tilting frame on the ramp. To prevent the trolleys slipping out of the frame, one of the women has to stand behind the frame and secure it with a broad wooden beam. Sometimes the dented trolleys have to be removed from the frame with a crowbar. Everyone's sweating underneath their prison garb or Wehrmacht uniform despite the cold, and still there's more coal coming out of the shaft. In the end, they spend ten hours shuffling trolleys and coal around before they stumble back to the camp, wolf down another portion of gruel and bread, and collapse in their bunks. They're too exhausted to talk and all fall asleep immediately.

~

When I was little, I loved to stay overnight at my grandparents' house. They had the fluffiest of all duvets, and pillows to match, and after dinner I used to put on my pyjamas, brush my teeth and snuggle into bed. Cilly would kiss me goodnight, and then tug gently on the fat pillow underneath my head, rocking it ever so slightly. I remember watching the continuous and hypnotising reflection of car headlights passing by the house in the small slit of window visible behind the almost-closed curtains, the earthen effigy of a crucified Jesus hanging over the door to the bedroom and Cilly's breathing. I felt safe and detached and happy and soon fell asleep, every time.

~

The next day it's the same. Wake-up call, roll call, a meagre breakfast, and then they're off to the mine, emptying trolleys. And the day after that. And after that. Their daily ration is four small pieces of dark rye bread, wet and sticky, divided into two portions for breakfast and supper plus a quarter-litre of black, unsweetened tea. For lunch, they have gruel or *kasha* made from millet or buckwheat, or some kind of watery potato mash without fat. If Cilly is lucky, there is a cabbage leaf, a few lonely lentils, peas with maggots or fish bones thrown in. Very rarely a teaspoon of sugar is handed out. They enjoy that treat: the women dip the wet bread into the sugar to make it last longer. The diet does not once make them feel full, and there is a constant nagging hunger in their insides every day. One morning, Cilly sees two prisoners in the mess hall delicately trying to pick up slivers of fish bone from the wooden tables with their wet fingertips. Everyone in the camps is suffering from the meagre rations, and the women are getting weaker each day. The morning always starts with the emaciated corpses of young women dragged out of the barracks by the still living occupants, stripped naked and put on a wooden trolley and carted off to a mass grave somewhere behind the fence. Two men from the male camp across the road have been chosen for this work, the so-called gravediggers, and no one is allowed to accompany them except an armed guard. One morning Cilly witnesses their work as she and Angelika walk to the mess hall. The dead lie this way and that on the trolley, their arms and legs dangling over the sides as the two men silently push it over the uneven and frozen parade ground towards the gate.

Escape is impossible. The camp is surrounded by a 3-metre wooden fence topped with barbed wire. In front of the main fence is a second one, made entirely of barbed wire. Beyond the wooden fence on all four corners of the camp are watchtowers, equipped with searchlights and manned by guards armed with machine guns. The guards are told to use their fire arms without warning if one of the prisoners leaves the camp without supervision. Inside the camp, there are separate areas for men and women, a hospital barracks for people sick with typhus and dysentery, a kitchen and attached mess hall and a barber. The whole atmosphere is intimidating, and the women wonder why the Soviet authorities are so afraid of them. Escape is hopeless anyway. They would have to traverse 2,000 kilometres without food, maps and, more importantly, without help. The camp entrance has a large double gate, covered with red banners in Russian letters. Right next to the gate is the guard barracks. This is where the prisoners' world ends.

Due to the inadequate diet, many people in the camp become sick: spotted fever, typhus, tuberculosis. Whoever succumbs to sickness receives their ration in the infirmary, through a trap in the door. The other prisoners are not allowed to enter, and there is no medical care, not even an attendant. In the bunk beneath Cilly and Angelika, a young woman from Danzig is sick. Claudia is a pretty blonde seamstress and was taken right off the pavement just after the Red Army marched into town. She was thin and weak when she arrived, and now she has faded to almost nothing. There are dark circles under her swollen eyes, and her cheekbones almost pierce her dry skin. She does not want to report as sick because she is afraid of being brought to the infirmary – most 'patients' simply die there after a day or two. Each morning she pushes herself to work, and the other women try to give her easy tasks or hide her behind disused trolleys where the foreman will not see her. But yesterday she took a turn for the worse: she can no longer breathe properly.

'I'm afraid,' she whispers to Cilly in the morning, 'please let me stay with you in the brigade.'

Angelika makes her open her mouth and discovers that her whole throat is covered with some sort of whitish fungus.

'Don't be afraid dear,' she says 'but rest for another five minutes. We'll bring you breakfast.'

'Diphtheria,' Angelika whispers to Cilly as they walk to the mess hall.

'I think we have to take her to the infirmary.'

'Let's wait another day,' Cilly says.

'We'll bring her to the roll call and after she's counted we'll hide her in the last row of bunks. The guards won't check there anyway and so she can rest for a day. Maybe that will help?'

Angelika sighs and kicks at the dirty snow.

'All right. I'll save a piece of bread for her.'

Claudia rests, and after returning from work at the mine that day Angelika roasts a piece of bread on the oven and gives it to her to eat, while Cilly holds her up and rubs the back of the wheezing woman. Claudia cannot speak but nods at them, trying to swallow bites of the bread, but her eyes go wide and she starts to cough violently, throwing up bread and blood and small bits of fungus. Angelika jumps aside and Cilly grabs Claudia, who is convulsing and twitching and has blood running from her mouth and tears pouring from her eyes. After a while she sinks to the side and falls asleep, weakly sobbing and coughing. She does not say a word to Cilly and Angelika. The next morning she is dead.

~

Sometimes I rub my face with both hands, just because it is too horrible and too far away and too long ago and I'll never be able to put it all into context. It still sounds like a dark fairy tale, something that happened in the Middle Ages or the Thirty Years' War, but nothing that happened to my bubbly grandmother and her friends. Let's get back to my train. I'm safer there.

Clack-clack, clack-clack, clack-clack. The next morning, very early and in semi-darkness, I'm woken by the sound of Tatyana and Vadim packing their bags and leaving our compartment. They are replaced by two young men who immediately slip into their bunks and start snoring. I go back to sleep as well.

Later, when I wake up, the sun is shining through our window and I can hear Yulia getting up. I wriggle out from under my blanket and, after a nod to Yulia, who is already preparing breakfast on her bunk, shuffle to the washroom for another cat lick. When I return to our compartment, I meet the *provodnitsa* in the corridor. She points at my socks and says something I don't understand, but her tone is disapproving. I smile and walk back to my compartment. I sit down on Yulia's bunk where she has cleared her bedding away and we start a hushed conversation, as our two new companions are still snoring in their bunks. Then the *provodnitsa* comes into our compartment and hands me a pair of disposable plastic slippers sealed in a plastic bag. She smiles and says something in Russian to Yulia, who laughs.

'You should not walk around Russian trains just in your socks,' she says. 'That's not the proper attire.'

I mumble a '*Spasibo*' and keep staring out of the window. The *provodnitsa* says something to Yulia and gestures at me to follow her. As I get up, Yulia translates: 'You want tea?'

And so, a few minutes later, I find myself back in my compartment sitting next to a young lady from Siberia in a pink tracksuit, with a glass of hot black tea in one hand, taken without milk as it is in Russia, and a sweet roll in the other. I look out of the window at the forest that has had us surrounded since I went to sleep eight hours ago. And even though I slept badly and in fits, right now I feel refreshed and awake, and no longer stressed by still being in a foreign country where I don't speak the language and can't read the signs.

The two men in the opposite bunk are still snoring when three men, naked but for shorts and flip-flops, enter our compartment. One of them has an enormous beer belly that flops over the waistband of his black shorts, the other two have the muscular build of construction workers. All have crude tribal and dragon tattoos on their shoulders and arms, and each carries a glass bottle of vodka and a large plastic bottle filled with a cloudy yellow liquid. They jovially wish us 'Good morning!' and are obviously already sozzled, despite the fact that it is not yet 11 in the morning, but they seem nice and unintimidating.

They start prodding the men in the opposite bunks until both sit up groaning, the blond man in the upper bunk only to immediately sink back down again, the black-haired man in the lower bunk to take a deep gulp from one of the vodka bottles. I am impressed – there's no way I could stomach that on waking up. The men sit down on the lower bunk and start chatting while taking sips from their bottles. The fat man offers his vodka to Yulia and me, but we both decline and sit back to read and write, respectively. After a minute or so of scribbling, one of the construction workers asks Yulia something and points at my notebook. I have explained the purpose of my journey to Yulia so she tells him that I'm a writer. The man laughs, but not in a negative way. He points at his chest, at me and my notebook while rapidly firing some more words at Yulia. 'He wants you to put him into your story. His name is Viktor.' Yulia laughs. I smile at the man and scribble something into my notebook. He nods, slaps my knee and offers me his vodka. Here is another stereotypical encounter straight from Lonely Planet, I think, a local offering me the regional firewater. It will soon be lunchtime, and I have planned to buy a beer at the next train station, so I ask Yulia to translate:

'I can't really drink vodka; my stomach does not react too well to it. I like to drink beer though.'

'Ha!' Viktor grabs one of the plastic bottles filled with yellow liquid from the fat man and pushes it into my hands. It looks like there are chunks of something grey floating around inside.

'This is old beer! Have a drink!'

Yulia shakes her head slightly as she translates.

'Thanks a lot Viktor, but I really can't. I'm just a stupid German who is not used to drinking before lunch.'

That makes Viktor smile, and I guess I have not insulted him by refusing his old beer.

After a while the man in the lower bunk and his three friends leave, waving at Yulia and me and their sleeping friend as they exit the compartment.

'It's good that you did not try his "beer",' Yulia says. 'When they run out of drink in some of the small towns and villages here, they sometimes just put all the dregs left in bottles after parties together in one bottle and call it "old beer". It's just a mix of leftovers, really.'

'Oh. Well, thanks for saving me from the stuff.'

If this book is ever translated into Russian, I hope that Viktor finds it and sees that I really did put him into my story, despite refusing his old beer.

I begin to understand the fascination of travelling on Russian trains, especially to Westerners. It's extremely slow, yet there is aways the feeling of movement and progression. Russians make themselves at home in their compartments and, due to the length of time you spend with them, you get to see more of their everyday behaviour and habits than, let's say, in two hours on the Eurostar or four hours on the German Inter City Express. Also, I'm not sweating too much thanks to the air conditioning. Only five hours left until Yekaterinburg, my final stop on this trip. Six more days in Russia. I am not having as many doubts as before, about what I will find and the imagined proto-Soviet people of Russia, but I'm still intimidated at the thought of putting Cilly's story next to mine, and at the immense expanse of Russia in which we might both get lost.

But do I feel closer to Cilly, now that it is only us two who made it this far? Yes. I carry her picture with me everywhere I go, and as I journey a part of me is keeping time with her, an inner eye conjuring her slow progress eastwards while I rest on my bunk or gaze out the window. I think I understand better now the immense involuntary journey she was forced to undertake. Of course, I have watched Gulag documentaries and read witness accounts of endless woods and lakes and steppes and 40 centimetres of snow, but often it's hard to differentiate between what I am watching or rading about and a thrilling action movie or paperback adventure. Often we make other people and the past real to us with the help of stereotypes and popular culture, and then are disillusioned when reality does not fulfil our expectations. But I now know it was anything but an adventure for her. Some survivors may have turned their experiences into adventures afterwards, as we travellers sometimes do when remembering only the good and not the boring parts of a trip. But even when creating their own narrative of their years in captivity for an audience, it was definitely no adventure while they were here. It was hunger and constant pain and fighting for survival. While my pampered, twenty-first-century Western European self may subconsciously crave extreme experiences, Cilly surely didn't. She would have preferred to stay in Lengainen.

And yet there is something appealing about 30 hours on the train. I've exhausted all the amusement potential my smartphone provides, written for two hours and read two chapters of my book; long ago I would have reached my destination anywhere in Central Europe. Here, I still have eight hours to go. So I spin out what's available, recharging my phone in the corridor of the carriage, watching the endless woods and the rain and the small, grey villages passing by the window for half an hour, an hour, two hours ... just because I have the time.

~

In the camp, alongside the gruelling work and pain and lack of food, there is the endless fight against lice. The lice prefer to sit in the seams of their clothing – all the seams of Cilly's woollen shirt are covered with lice, and it is impossible to kill all of them. They torture the prisoners, more merciless than any Soviet guard yet to be born.

A body lice infestation is treated by improving the personal hygiene of the infested person, including assuring a regular change of clean clothes. Clothing, bedding and towels used by the infested person should be laundered using hot water and machine dried using the hot cycle. A temperature of 54 degrees Celsius for five minutes will kill most lice and prevent eggs from hatching. Medication, insecticide or burning of clothing and bedding is usually not necessary, as the problem normally goes away with daily bathing, weekly laundering and drying of clothing, bedding, towels, etc. in a hot clothes dryer. There is no clothes dryer anywhere near the camps in Russia in 1945, and no immediate possibility of taking a bath.

At first Cilly perceives the lice on her body as simple parasites whose presumption makes her indignant. The way they dig their ugly grey-brown bodies into the pores of her skin revolts her. In the morning before marching off to work she takes great pleasure in holding a lighted candle and working it slowly up the seams of her clothes where the insects lurk. Usually their deaths are silent, though occasionally she hears a satisfying crackle. She does Angelika's clothes for her too, because Angelika does not have the necessary delicacy of hand and is liable to set fire to her underwear. If there is no candle available, a fiercely applied thumbnail is also effective. There is a sense of relief when some of the creatures are gone, like the crushing of a blood-gorged mosquito. Cilly, like most of the women, scratches almost all the time, but gradually becomes less aware that she is doing so. By the time they reach the mine, Cilly feels the first irritation on her skin. Within three hours, the heat of her working body hatches the eggs of hundreds of lice that are lying dormant in the seams of her shirt. By the time she reaches her barracks in the evening, her skin is once again alive with them.

~

All of a sudden, after several more hours of woods and small villages passing by the train window, I arrive. I say goodbye to Yulia and the two revellers in the opposite bunks and step off the train, awkwardly inching my luggage past the two *provodnitsas* standing at the train door, who bid me farewell with a friendly pat on the back. Another idiot tourist delivered to the middle of Russia. Well, not the middle, precisely. But further away from home than I've ever been before in my life.

8 YEKATERINBURG IS SVERDLOVSK

We think we have freedom of choice, but really most of our actions are puny meanderings in the prison yard built by history and early experience.

Anthony Loyd, *My War Gone By, I Miss It So*

Yekaterinburg is Russia's fourth-largest city, the administrative centre of Sverdlovsk Oblast, with a population of roughly 1.3 million, and the main industrial and cultural centre of the area. Between 1924 and 1991, the city was named Sverdlovsk after local Communist party leader Yakov Sverdlov.

Like Nizhny Tagil, Yekaterinburg is a young city in European terms. It was founded in 1723 by explorers Vasily Tatishchev and Georg Wilhelm de Gennin, a German, and named after Czar Peter the Great's wife Catherine I (Yekaterina). And like Nizhny Tagil, the city was one of Russia's first industrial cities, with development starting immediately after its foundation following decrees from the Czar that called for the establishment of metalworking businesses here.

But I'm not here for dead czars or iron ore. After Nizhny Tagil, Cilly spent all her remaining time in the Soviet Union in the Sverdlovsk area; it's also from here that she took her train back to Germany in 1949. She might have been marched along the streets of this city. During the 1930s, Yekaterinburg was one of several places developed by the Soviet government as a centre of heavy industry, during which time the large Uralmash factory and neighbourhood was built. As throughout the Urals, during World War II many state institutions and whole factories were relocated to Yekaterinburg, away from war-affected areas near the German advance, with many factories and their workers staying in Yekaterinburg after the victory in 1945. It was also home to approximately 30 Gulag and Gupvi main camps and even more *lagpunkts*; small agricultural, wood and factory camps. After her time in Nizhny Tagil, Cilly spent three years near Sverdlovsk, including two and a half years on a farm and forest camp in the small village of Kosulino, and the rest of her time in Russia near what is today the industrial town of Revda. I plan to visit both places.

Yekaterinburg main station does not look like much. Brown buildings and storage areas connected by aerial wires line the tracks and platform. I follow the other arriving passengers to the exit, lugging my bag over my shoulder. I know roughly where I need to go: to the metro and the city centre. As an important industrial centre and transport hub, the city grew very rapidly in the 1970s and 1980s, and in 1980 construction of the city metro began. On 26 April 1991, the sixth metro in Russia and the 13th in the Soviet Union – which ceased to exist only a few months later – was finally opened to the public. It's not as impressive as the neo-Gothic stations of the Moscow metro, and instead of utilising fancy multilingual vending machines I have to buy my tickets from a stony-faced booking clerk. The ticket is just a blank metal coin that I insert in the gates to the escalator, which leads down to the platform. The metro in Yekaterinburg is also air-conditioned, cooled to 20 degrees, and I cross my fingers and hope I can avert a cold. The trains are almost as spacious as the Moscow ones, and I rumble from the station to Ploschschad 1905 Goda station. Here I promptly get lost and walk in the wrong direction after emerging back into the sun, past the city hall and the Lenin statue opposite.

After getting my bearings, I walk along Lenina Street, the six-lane main road that runs through Yekaterinburg. It feels like walking into a Turkish bath. It's a humid, muggy, 36 de-

13 *Yekaterinburg, Russia*

grees Celsius and the grey sky seems to hang just above our heads. I pass a few street vendors selling drinks and ice cream and, strangely, a group of scantily clad women in purple bikinis dancing to loud house music on the cargo platform of a large truck. But I am no longer trying to fathom the weirder cultural aspects of Russia, and shrug. To my left is what looks like a large pond, and the bridge I'm walking on is actually a dam for the banked-up River Iset, which flows on to my right through a small park. Concrete embankments guide the river's flow, so people can sit on the banks and promenade in a straight line. At the far end of the park is some sort of spire or obelisk crowned by a statue commemorating I don't know what. Somebody has set an empty bottle of champagne on the handrail of the dam, in line with the obelisk, and I consider the strange arrangement a good omen.

Further on, there's another square with a small wooden tower and a bronze statue of the two city founders, clad in eighteenth-century frontiersman attire. The tower is a restored remnant from the city's past as a frontier town, an old water tower. There is not much of a frontier feeling today, but I already like Yekaterinburg better than Moscow. Despite its size, the area I'm walking through has a proper city centre feeling and seems to cater more to pedestrians. Even the main road has only six lanes, and plenty of pedestrian crossings. I contemplate taking one of the clanking trams that saunter past, but despite the heat and my heavy bags, I'm eager to get an understanding of the lie of the land. So I shuffle on, past a small chapel, colourful shops and the impressive 1960s brutalist post office towards the main building of the university, complete with Yakov Sverdlov statue, and the impressive nineteenth-century opera house opposite my hotel.

The hotel is called Iset, and it is large and white with ten floors. It looks almost menacing, located directly on the main road next to a roundabout and squinting down at passing cars. It has a semi-circular shape with one wing sticking out – from above, you'd be able to see that the hotel is shaped in the form of a hammer and sickle. Planned and executed as a fine example of constructivist architecture, it was the local headquarters of the NKVD and KGB until it became a hotel in 1961. I find it somewhat disconcerting that I might sleep in one of the former rooms of Cilly's jailers, but I shoulder my bag and walk inside. The concierge is very friendly, even though he looks a bit put out when I tell him that my hotel in Moscow did not properly register me with the authorities. I don't mind him keeping my passport, and take the lift to my hotel room. I let my bag fall upon the bed and ignore the brown 1980s interior. There is a desk and an empty fridge, and from the window, I look down on the tree-lined main road and over tall apartment buildings and shopfronts covered with adverts. In the distance there are large dark clouds towering over factory chimneys painted with red stripes. I decide to go and buy beer for the fridge.

The Iset is the perfect base for my stay in Yekaterinburg: it is near the tram lines, has an off-licence in the basement and, even more importantly, is the home of one of Boris Yeltsin's favourite restaurants: Uralskiie Pelmeni. And if there is one food I have learned to love on this trip, it's dumplings – pierogi and pelmeni. Dumplings are also pretty cheap, which is fortunate. Slowly but surely I am running out of money.

~

Cilly's 22nd birthday is on 21 April 1945. There is still snow on the ground and it is freezing. They have no clocks and no calendars, but there are some expert inmates, mostly senior POWs and a few elderly women, who know the exact date, and through the position of the sun they can guess the time of day. So Cilly asks these prisoners from time to time and makes notches in the side of her bunk to keep track of time, and then one day she realises that she has turned a year older. She is tired all the time and caught in the small universe of sleep, breakfast, roll call, work, lunch, work, dinner, sleep, without any hope of escape. For a brief moment she remembers her 22nd birthday the year before. She celebrated with her family, with her brothers and her older sisters, who with their husbands had come from Allenstein to the farm. They had cake and coffee and there were questions from her older sisters as to why she was still working on the farm with no husband in sight, but maybe that was what Cilly wanted, to run the farm with her brothers. Another trolley comes rumbling up from the pit, and she pushes it towards the ramp with three other women, cursing the bloody Russians and Hitler at the same time. This is how she spends her birthday – with tears in her eyes, pushing a trolley filled with coal, hungry, freezing and behind barbed wire.

A couple of weeks after her birthday, spring arrives. Snow and ice on the roads are replaced by mud and dust, especially at the mine where the coal dust is no longer kept down by layers of snow. Every trolley emptied onto the wagons wraps the women in black ash clouds, so they have started to cover their faces with rags and old scarves, but still the coal dust seeps into every pore and they all look old and wrinkled under the layers of dirt and coal. But there are birds in the air, and, when the sun is shining, even grey, smoky Nizhny Tagil looks almost pleasant.

One morning, as they stand on the parade ground in front of the barracks for the roll call of the day, Cilly hears firecrackers in the distance. She looks at Angelika.

'Have you heard that?'

'The shooting? Yes.'

Cilly looks around, and yes, it's shooting, not firecrackers. Despite having witnessed the effects of war on East Prussia just months before, she has not heard a gun fired in Russia until now. And it is getting louder. The other women hear it too, and they flinch and duck as the shooting nears the camp. The two guards with clipboards who are doing the roll call also hear it, and one lets his clipboard fall to the ground and grabs the rifle slung over his back. Suddenly there's another guard running towards them down the road from the male camp, a young man without a gun and with a red face, out of breath, laughing and whooping. He pushes open the gate, and while he runs towards the two guards and the women he shouts at the top of his lungs:

'*Gitler kapuut, Woina kapuut, skorro domoi!*' – 'Hitler is finished, the war is finished, and soon we go home!'

He comes to a skidding halt in front of the two other guards and hugs them and slaps their shoulders, laughing. Some of the women understand and start to laugh and cry too, others turn to Cilly who has to translate until everyone has heard the news and everyone is laughing and shouting and hugging each other. The guards on the watchtowers start shooting their rifles and machine guns into the air and all is noise and happiness. The guards slap the women's backs and tell them that yes, they might be going home soon.

This is Wednesday 9 May 1945. The night before, on 8 May, the unconditional surrender of all German forces in Europe has been signed by supreme German military commander Wilhelm Keitel, Soviet Marshal Georgy Zhukov and representatives of the western Allies. Since the Soviet Union is to the east of Germany, it was 9 May Moscow time when the surrender took effect here, and it takes a while for the news to travel east and reach Nizhny Tagil. World War II in Europe is over.

The smiling guards let the women celebrate for a while, and everyone on the parade ground harbours the feeling that it must surely be over soon, that they will get back to Allenstein, Temeschburg, Vienna soon. But after an hour or so a stern-faced officer walks into the yard with a clipboard, and reprimands the guards. After some shouting, the prisoner column sets off towards the mine again, and no more cheering is to be heard. Only then, when they're trudging back to work after the earth-shattering news, does Cilly realise the full extent of her predicament with a clarity she did not possess before. The Russians will need the prisoners to keep working – it will be a while before the Red Army soldiers return home, and judging from the four years that the French POWs worked on her own farm she understands that their stay here is not for months, but years. She realises that she will need all her strength to make it through the day and the next and the one after that. Whatever it takes her to get home, she will do it. She has not succumbed to desperation in the past, and she will not do it now. They will not break and kill her. She conjures up the image of her mother and Monika, of the lake in the summer sun. She will return there one day.

But that is not now. Now, World War II has ended, and she still has almost four years in Russia ahead of her.

~

All the contemporary witnesses I talked with confirmed that in their first year in the camps there were three things and three things only: hunger, exhaustion, death. There was no interest in their wider surroundings, in why Nizhny Tagil was there and why they ended up here – there was no spare time. The prisoners tried to make it through each day on their meagre rations, wolfed down their dinners in the evenings and fell into their bunks. There were some hushed conversations during work hours, but mostly the women who got to know each other on the transports clung together where possible; there was no energy left to make new acquaintances. In addition, there was no improvement in the supply situation after the war in Europe ended in May 1945 – it even got worse, both for prisoners and all other citizens living in the Soviet Union. A famine in 1946 devastated Ukraine, the former breadbasket of the USSR: 28,000 villages and 30,000 farms had been ruined by the war, and there were not enough people capable of working. Hundreds of thousands of men had died, and demobilisation from the army was still ongoing. The famine in Ukraine reached its peak in the first half of 1947: it killed (according to the data of various researchers) anywhere between 100,000 and 2.8 million people, mainly Ukrainian peasants and farmers. Even the Soviet capital Moscow suffered severe supply shortages – so no wonder that the German prisoners of war literally ended up at the bottom of the food chain. If the Russian people had nothing, they had less.

~

'There is no way we can fulfil this quota. This is madness.'

Cilly shakes her head and looks at Angelika and Rosemarie, a 17-year-old who was taken from Insterburg. The foreman has just declared that their daily quota of emptied trolleys is not enough and that they need to empty at least ten more each day. The women themselves never count how many trolleys they empty, and no one dares to ask what the exact number is.

'*Dawai!* Let's go to work and there will be an extra ration of bread when you return tonight,' the foreman says and walks towards his small office in the main building near the mine, while their two guards start pushing the women towards the trolleys that have just ridden up, spilling over with coal.

Cilly takes heart. 'But how many trolleys do we have to empty?' she shouts at the passing foreman. His head jerks up and he stares at her. Cilly considers staring back for a moment, but then Rosemarie pulls her away. The foreman smiles.

They don't fulfil the quota. When it turns dark they march back to the camp, the thought of their piece of bread moving them forwards. The way through the forest of factories is always a long one, and it seems to get longer the more exhausted they get. Elderly prisoners sometimes sit down against walls to rest, but there is a high chance of falling asleep and being woken up by kicks from the guards, who herd the exhausted people back into the column with constant curses and threats. After reaching the camp, the prisoners return their tools to the shed and go to get their evening ration. Sometimes they roast pieces of bread in the oven to fight against diarrhoea. After eating they just exist in a sort of coma, awaiting the beginning of the next shift in the morning, not even really noticing the lice any more. With the demanding work, their meagre rations aren't enough to keep them alive but they somehow keep them from dying too, Cilly thinks when she has to push herself out of her bunk in the mornings with an already rumbling stomach and a feeling of light-headedness. Their guards tell them constantly that they have to rebuild what the German soldiers destroyed, but she wonders why they do not feed the prisoners properly, if their work is so essential. May turns into June then July then August, and although the weather is warm and the sun sometimes shines, the sunlight and blue sky do not bring joy with them.

In the camp, one of Cilly's greatest fears is of falling into the pit. Their toilet is a latrine pit covered with two planks, set in a corner of the camp beneath one of the guard towers, barely hidden behind thin shrubs. There is no handrail, and you have to balance your bare behind between the two planks. In winter it was not so bad as the urine and faeces froze immediately, but now in summer the smell is unbearable. The planks are smeared with mud, urine and excrement, and whoever is sick and weak is in danger of losing their balance and falling into the pit. Doris and the other kitchen workers also dump the kitchen slops in there, fish heads and the like. One morning, Cilly sees two women from her barracks fabricate some sort of instrument, a long pole with a nail at the top, and with it they gather the fish heads from the pit. They eat the fish bones and leftovers, but most other women decline when they are offered a share. Later, she sees the women being carried to the infirmary by their comrades, one of them projectile vomiting a thin brown broth onto the frozen ground.

One day as they return from the mine and sit down for gruel and bread, Doris comes over and sits down next to Angelika and Cilly. Both look at her expectantly, as this is something she has never done before in the evening. Doris stares at her dirty hands and sighs.

'Something happened today. Do you remember Frank, the lanky prisoner they made one of the gravediggers?'

'The one who always looked like he had forgotten something?' Cilly says.

'Yes, that one. This morning, after you left for work, they brought a few corpses from barracks four to the graveyard, and afterwards he went to the latrine. He slipped and fell. No one heard him shouting. The guards on the tower saw nothing and only found him after roll call when they thought he had tried to escape and started searching for him. His arm was sticking out of the pit and the other gravedigger had to pull him out. The poor man drowned in shit.'

Doris sighs again and rises up from the table.

'Be careful when you go there, will you?'

'Cilly and I will only go together from now on,' Angelika says and takes a bite from her bread.

In September, they are taken off the trolleys and instead marched off to work in a tractor factory. Thankfully, it is 3 kilometres' march instead of the usual 4 to the mine. Here, they also work ten-hour shifts, day and night shifts in rotation, and each shift without food. Their work is to screw metal plates to larger metal plates with old and oily screwdrivers, all day long, 14 screws in each plate and then they are handed the next. The prisoners receive food in the morning and once they return to the camp. After each shift, they are so tired that they can hardly move the spoon to their lips. They have to work every day, including weekends. When the factory is closed for a Soviet bank holiday, the prisoners clean public latrines or lay train tracks. Once bubbly, Cilly has become silent and shut away in herself, like most of the women. It is as if by keeping silent they can save energy, wordlessly trotting through the grey streets of Nizhny Tagil every morning and evening.

~

I venture out into colourful Yekaterinburg again. The streets are wide and there are lots of green spaces in town. It finally feels like I've reached a proper city with people lounging in parks and sitting on the terraces of cafes filled with second-hand furniture and dog-eared books, a world away from the stifling hectic pressure of Moscow. I buy a coffee at a nearby cafe, with outside seating on a wooden terrace with a few white

pieces of cloth hanging from the beamed roof helping to obscure the traffic on nearby Lucharnaskogo Street. It caters to a
young hip crowd, and feels more pleasant than almost anything I have encountered in Russia so far. I spend an hour here,
sipping my coffee and reading a book, and decide that I am no
longer intimidated by the country. Afterwards I walk to the
nearby army museum, only to find it closed, past a small
square with a giant black statue of a Red Army soldier kneeling
and resting his right arm on a Kalashnikov, and down a long
alley with chestnut trees on both sides. Turning a corner just
before my hotel, I spot a piece of street art I haven't seen before:
a mosaic of the iconic image of Red Army soldiers hoisting the
Soviet flag over the Reichstag in Berlin in 1945, consisting of
hundreds of other small black-and-white images from World
War II. But this is nothing official, no repurposed Soviet memorial. Like the anchor graffiti and replicas of propaganda
posters in Warsaw, this is smaller, personal: the spectre of the
Great Patriotic War, as World War II is called in Russia, still
firing the imagination of my generation and the ones after.
Again, I'm surprised by the city.

My next stop is the Cathedral on the Blood, or, to be more
accurate, The Church on Blood in Honour of All Saints Resplendent in the Russian Land. It is a colourful Orthodox
church with golden domes, built on the site of Ipatiev House
in Yekaterinburg, where Nicholas II, the last Czar of Russia,
his family and several servants were shot by the Bolsheviks.
The church commemorates the Romanovs' sainthood, as the
family was canonised by the Orthodox church in 2000. Yakov
Sverdlov, the man who gave the city its name, allegedly carried
out Lenin's order to kill the Czar and his family, only to perish
from the flu a few months after the Romanovs died. Fate is inexorable, some say.

From the cathedral, I follow a red line painted on the pavement to the Old Town. The 'Red Line' is a tourist route that
traces a walking path around the centre of Yekaterinburg.

Thanks to the efforts of volunteers, 35 of the best architectural sights, historical places, unusual monuments and viewpoints have been chosen and connected with a red line drawn on asphalt, which forms a circular walking route through the centre of town. I follow the line through a quiet area with beautiful old wooden houses on both sides, proper frontier houses with yards enclosed by wooden fences, some with the restored double eagle of Czarist Russia still sitting over the door. And then, in the sunshine, for the first time in Russia I have a feeling of understanding, of getting a glimpse of the country and its history of slaughter and oppression, of beauty and resilience.

～

On their way from the camp to the tractor factory, Cilly and the other female prisoners march past two camps of Russian criminals – at least this is what the guards tell them. These are Soviet Gulags, which contain not only criminals but also political prisoners and former Russian prisoners of war.

These former POWs have been betrayed by Stalin twice: many Soviet prisoners who survived the deadly German captivity (Russian prisoners who were considered 'subhuman' by the Nazis were deliberately left to starve by the Wehrmacht, in contrast to British and American POWs) were accused by the Soviet authorities of collaborating with the Nazis or branded as traitors under Order No. 270, which prohibited any Red Army soldier from surrendering to the enemy. During and after World War II, Soviet POWs freed from German camps by the advancing Red Army went to special 'filtration' camps, where some were cleared and sent home, but many others arrested again and condemned to serve in penal battalions and labour camps. Later in 1945, more filtration camps were set up for repatriated so-called *Ostarbeiter*, slave workers the Wehrmacht had brought to Germany against their will, and other displaced persons, and these camps processed more than 4 million people.

Sometimes it happens that the column of German women is overtaken by a column of Russian prisoners – they are made to march even faster than the Germans. Cilly's column has to step to the side of the road to let them overtake, and if the women do not pay attention it sometimes happens that some-one from the prisoner column grabs their fur cap, or a shawl – which is then lost forever. One day while they are standing by the side of the road, one of the prisoners grabs not just a hat, but one of the smaller women. He just lifts her up and drags her along. Cilly and the other women don't realise what is hap-pening at first, but when the woman bites the arm of her cap-tor, he cries out and she falls down. The woman stumbles through the mass of men back to the female column and into the arms of her comrades. When the guards realise what has happened, they start shouting and fire their rifles in the air. The whole column of Russian prisoners then have to go down on their knees and shuffle past the German column as collec-tive punishment. Maybe the fellow was only playing around, but when another group of Russian prisoners passes them two days later, Cilly sees the small woman step back to the other side of their column.

Once every three or four weeks, the women are allowed a bath, the *banja* they had already experienced on their train journey. The guards take them to a small shed in a neighbour-ing camp where they take all their clothes off and are allowed to scrub and wash themselves with lukewarm water, not hot enough to kill the lice but at least providing some sense of cleanliness for the women. Cilly also receives a new canteen and a spoon for gathering her food rations, and her spoon is the only tool and piece of cutlery she possesses. It is made from cheap steel; the handle is shaped like a knife with a sharp edge on the one side and the other side a spoon, with a short wooden grip in the middle. So when they receive the occasional potato, she is glad that she can cut it like a civilised person and has no need to chomp on it while holding it in her dirty hands. A prisoner always keeps her spoon with her; this is what she has learned. You never know when you might find something edible, or just edible, which needs cutting.

As she gets weaker, Cilly cannot concentrate properly, and working is increasingly difficult. The prisoners are constantly slipping or banging their heads or cutting themselves, so everyone is bruised and their hands and faces are covered with dirty bandages. One day it happens – while tightening a screw, the screwdriver slips and Cilly cuts the palm of her hand with the oil-covered blade. There is no time to wash the wound, as the next piece of metal is being brought up by two other women and the guards are watching her, so she just takes off her dirty scarf and wraps it around her palm. Within a few hours, her hand is infected, swollen and causing her enormous throbbing pain. She tries to ignore it, but it is so bad she cannot sleep that night. After two days, she shows it to Doris in the mess hall.

'I'm afraid they'll send me to the sick barracks.'

'They might. But we can do something about it.'

Doris takes her to the kitchen and washes her hand under hot water in the sink, and then gets a razor blade from a cupboard that she washes in hot water, too. Cilly swallows, but the pain is bad and her fear of the infirmary even worse. Doris grips the razor and looks at her.

'This will hurt like hell, but only once. Hold still!'

Cilly doesn't look, so she doesn't pull her hand away when the razor is nearing. Then the razor cuts into the swollen red and yellow flesh and she howls and howls, Doris gripping her hand and arm hard and letting the pus run out together with the blood. Cilly slumps down on a wooden stool while Doris patches her up, her hand no longer throbbing, and the pain replaced with the sharp sting of the cut.

'Come back tomorrow morning and I'll change the dressing. Don't show it to the guards.'

Cilly is glad that she has friends like Angelika and Doris,

older women she can rely on. Doris is also lucky insofar as she is posted in the kitchen, and is a veteran of the camps. She is from the Banat, a region of Serbia and Romania that is inhabited by ethnic Germans, and which had been reached by the Red Army in September 1944, so it became one of the first areas where the Soviet authorities applied their policy of 'mobilising and interning' German civilians. Doris reached Nizhny Tagil in October 1944, six months before the transports from East Prussia arrived.

At the end of September, the first snow starts to fall and within days it is winter again. Sometimes there are snowstorms as fierce as hurricanes. If such a storm suddenly breaks out when the women are working in the factory, the march back is increasingly difficult – they cannot see their hands in front of their faces due to the howling whiteness and cold wind cutting at their eyes. Sometimes work brigades get lost and it takes them hours to return to the camp. In November 1945 a child is born: Rosemarie, captured pregnant in East Prussia, gives birth to a daughter in the camp. The others approach Angelika,

14 *Camp in Nizhny Tagil*

who they know is well versed in the Bible, to christen the child. She is reluctant at first, but there are no priests, so in the end she relents. In a small parlour in the barracks that the other prisoners have created by hanging up sack linen around two bunk beds, which they stole from one of the factories, they celebrate a simple baptism for the child, who is called Eva-Maria. And despite the rationing, the small child lives. All they see around them day in, day out is hunger and death, and here a tiny human is born amidst the desperation.

The child and her mother return to Germany with one of the first sick transports. And this is no surprise – as opposed to children born in the Gulag, who were allowed to stay with their mothers or who were looked after in camp nurseries, children and mothers in the Gupvi camps were considered too weak to help rebuild the USSR and were sent home. As Stefan Karner writes in *Im Archipel GUPVI*:

> The first [...] prisoners were already released in 1945/46. These were mainly – as mentioned before – sick, invalid or long-term unfit persons, thereby such who could not be used for rebuilding the Soviet Union – always under the premise that the prisoner had not partaken in war crimes.

In November, Rosemarie and Eva-Maria return to East Prussia, on a train filled with sick prisoners too weak to work. In the same month, Cilly and her brigade are brought to yet another workplace, three hours' march from the camp, where they have to cut peat on the outskirts of town. They work alongside train tracks, and the Russians bring trolleys that they fill with the peat. They have to work over Christmas as well, in shifts: eight to noon, noon to four o'clock. And Cilly's group has to work until eight in the evening. *'Bistra na rabotu!* Back to work!' the guards shout at the prisoners, as they stand in a circle around the fire. As she sighs and picks up her spade again, Cilly thinks that at home she would have gone to Christmas Mass around this time. Her first two Christmas Days in Russia are filled with work as usual, but without food. They do not receive any rations at all, no one knows why. So they just return to the barracks and lie down in their bunks. All their thoughts are with home, but they do not know if there is a home left. The women from Berlin talk of falling bombs, the women from East Prussia and Silesia of burning farms. They have no news from their families, no news at all except that the war has ended. After a while Angelika weakly tries to sing a Christmas carol, *Stille Nacht, Heilige Nacht*, Silent Night, Holy Night, and a few women join in, but after a while the meagre chorus dies out and the women just lie on their bunks crying, hoping in vain that they still might receive a piece of bread before they fall asleep with growling stomachs.

~

Is there a better time for having a grandmother than at Christmas? On Christmas Eve, which is when the main celebrations happen in Germany and the presents are exchanged, my parents would drop me and my brother off at Cilly and Willy's in order to have time to prepare our house for Christmas dinner in the evening. We would be positioned on the sofa, with the usual ubiquity of food heaped upon us. Sometimes we would watch the Christmas TV programmes with my grandfather in his armchair, while Cilly was busying herself in the kitchen and dining room. Sometimes we would set up the large model railway and trains that my grandfather collected, with miniature stations, tracks and a variety of electric and coal locomotives, which we drove in loops over the table in the dining room, my brother and I fighting over control of the dynamo that regulated the speed of the trains. Afterwards, we would play cards with my grandparents, a game called *Mau Mau* where we were allowed to bet with small copper ten-Pfennig pieces, which my grandfather would gather, chuckling, after each round, having beaten his grandchildren at cards. It would slowly turn dark outside, and we would retire to the living room to watch TV, munching crisps and chocolate washed down with glasses of cold milk.

Once back at our house, we would sit down for Christmas dinner first, Cilly helping my mother to prepare and serve the food. I remember her tutting from time to time and remarking on food she did not like or the layout of the crockery and cutlery, but I never remember there being a big fight on Christmas Eve. After dinner and dessert, my brother and I would stare at the cigarette my father would always smoke, because we knew that once he finished there would be PRESENTS. Then, at some point, my mother would ring a bell and we were allowed to enter the living room, where the tree was lit with candles and our presents were piled underneath. What followed was the frantic ripping of wrapping paper and exclamatory jubilation upon discovering another item from our wish lists. After that frenzy, things settled down a bit, and we started building our Lego spaceships, Carrera speedways or He-Man castles, my father on the floor with us building and playing, Cilly and Willy watching on, sipping glasses of wine or cognac. I now wonder if their thoughts sometimes went back to other Christmases, those during the war and those spent in captivity.

The next day, Christmas Day, was traditionally spent at my grandparents' house. Cilly was very particular about it, about the crisp starched tablecloth, the crockery, the wines. Mostly sweet German white wines from the Moselle accompanied my grandmother's traditional Christmas dishes: turkey with a delicious brown gravy or roast pork swimming in a creamy sauce. There would be potatoes and green beans on the side, but I was happy stuffing myself with pieces of turkey breast and lean slices of pork. Dessert was always vanilla ice cream smothered in red cherry sauce, and I loved that too. Sometimes we were allowed a nap afterwards, but mostly we would sit in front of the TV or play cards again or even Nine Men's Morris, but I was never bored or unhappy or lost then, sitting in the warmth with a full belly and the murmur of the adults washing over me while I played with one of the new toys I had brought with me. Sometimes my grandfather would grab me and snuggle with me, or Cilly would plant a wet kiss on my forehead when walking past with the dishes, wearing an apron. Most of her beliefs in social order and proper behaviour had been eroded by then – when my father was a child, Cilly made him walk to Christmas Mass after dinner, but she never did this with us. Like most grandparents, she was softer with us than she had been with her own children. If the camps had made her hard, I never knew her that way.

Later, when I grew older, I felt differently about our Christmas rituals. When for the first time I celebrated Christmas away from my family, I felt a little relieved. Relief was not what Cilly felt during her Soviet Christmases, that's one thing I am sure of now. And I now wish I had spent more time with her and Willy, later in life. I do remember one particular Christmas Day when I was older though: my brother and I had partied the night before, going out to the only club open in Solingen on Christmas Eve, dancing ironically to Wham! and chasing shots with beer. At Cilly's house, we both fell asleep right after stuffing ourselves with lunch, leaning against one another on the sofa in front of the TV. Cilly got up from the table to get a blanket from the bedroom, tucked us in and put two small pillows behind our heads, as if we were seven years old again.

In Yekaterinburg, my phone rings.

'Marcel? It's Johnny. I have bad news.'

I had rented out my apartment in Berlin to my friend Johnny and his girlfriend while I was away, and he now tells me that my gas at home has been switched off and the two were forced to shower with cold water for two days. They are leaving on the day he calls me, so it's not a problem for them, but I wonder what went wrong. For the first time in weeks, I check my bank account online and find out that I am in trouble. Thanks to a disastrous miscalculation, I'm currently stranded about 3,500 kilometres from home with almost no money left and the sole hope that my credit card will hold out. I decide to switch to emergency money-saving mode, relying on the hotel breakfast and cheap Soviet-style canteens. But maybe, just a tiny maybe, this imagined twentieth-century hardship might bring me a bit closer to Cilly. There are no guards maltreating me or handing out watery soup, but my bank account may take on the form of a threatening presence hovering over me and dictating my moves up to a certain point. So it does perversely seem fitting; looking at a coffee table book of photos of the local countryside at the tourist office, I felt stupid for not having organised a trip to a nearby lake or the mountains. But then, Cilly didn't take a leisurely trip to a lake or to the mountains when she was here; the only outdoor activity she got was chopping wood in the forest and harvesting turnips in the fields in autumn. But she must have felt something, being outside. Since she was used to working with and living from the land, I imagine she would have learned to read the seasons and the land here in the Urals. Still, she was in captivity one way or another during that time, wherever she was.

9 KOLKHOZ

It was more my mind-set than geographical position that accounted for my feeling of isolation. It was not necessarily a bad sensation, indeed at times I relished the liberty of my solitude.

Anthony Loyd, *My War Gone By, I Miss It So*

After she came to West Germany, Cilly became a city dweller, and never returned to the agricultural lifestyle of East Prussia. With her arrival in West Germany, her life became thoroughly urban. There was however one thing she started as soon as possible: a garden. Cilly and Willy acquired an allotment near their house in Solingen, and for many years they spent most of their summers there. They grew peas, beans and lettuces, built an extension to the existing shed, set up plastic fences to replace the old wooden ones. During summer school holidays, I used to visit them often. I chased spiders with my dad, helped my grandfather build small stone walls around new beds and was fed strawberries and cream, sugar snap peas, and chocolate by Cilly. Even though the allotment was the last one in the garden settlement, right next to a stinking creek that was fed from a nearby drain, and the toilet was a hole in the back shed that you 'flushed' with water from a bucket, they loved it and so did I. At home we only had a balcony and my parents weren't remotely green-fingered when I was a child, so Cilly's allotment was my first ever contact with gardening and growing plants.

Arriving early in the morning, Cilly would open the small hut where they kept a gas stove and a fridge, and I was given some bitter lemonade while she boiled water for coffee. I would then sit down in the sun with comics or books while she was busy weeding. Sometimes I was allowed to throw the dead snails into the creek; they had died a drunkard's death in the small bowls of beer Cilly and Willy had set out around the beds the night before. My parents would often arrive around lunchtime or later in the afternoon, and then there would be coffee and cake, either outside under the apple tree we were allowed to climb, or under the big canopy if the weather was bad. Plum cake, strawberry cake and cream, coffee and beer. We would have a barbecue from time to time, and an old neighbour would visit and bring me sugar snap peas from his garden. I loved to peel the tiny green balls from their jackets and stuff them in my mouth, and they tasted sweet and bitter. I wonder if Cilly thought of her farm then, sitting at a rickety table on the lawn, laughing, in one of her aprons with her legs stretched out, watching her family eat and drink and talk around her.

In the evenings, we would pack all our stuff into bags and baskets, and the whole caravan of the Krueger family would set off from the end of the garden settlement to the family car parked outside the main gate. Cilly and Willy would walk home.

~

In Russia, they send her to the forest. It is July 1946, and in the camp in Nizhny Tagil no one really works; the prisoners are simply too weak. The guards don't make them work because they know the prisoners have no energy left, and so the women just linger around the camp, silently lying in their bunks and staring into nothingness, or listlessly sitting in the sun outside their barracks when the weather permits. They are starving. Of 1,500 prisoners in the two camps, around 100 go out for three or four hours a day to bring in any supplies that might be available.

During this period, Cilly's weight drops to only 45 kilograms. Sometimes, when she has to get up to walk to the mess
hall to receive her daily rations, everything goes black for a few
seconds because she is so weak from hunger and her blood
pressure can't cope with the sudden movement. One summer
morning, there is another roll call, and the women are surprised by the sound of approaching lorries as they are walking
to breakfast. A long row of trucks rumbles down the road from
the male camp, and the women ask themselves if that is it, if
they are finally going to be allowed to go home. But no – after
breakfast, they are told to gather their belongings, herded onto
the trucks and the convoy sets off. They are going to the forest.

I wonder if Cilly felt better when she realised they were
sending her to the fields and forests. This is something she
knew, much better than screwing metal plates together in factories or pushing coal trolleys. I imagine that it helped her, in
the beginning. But it would become the place in Russia that
almost killed her.

The trucks rumble past factories, camps and grey apartment buildings and then enter the open countryside. After
three or four hours' drive past fields and villages, they enter a
dark forest, where no other human settlements are visible.

'Damn it Cilly, I wonder where they are taking us this time!'
Angelika whispers. 'Do you think they are taking us to the
woods to shoot us?'

Before Cilly can answer, the trucks stop in front of their
new camp.

Kolkhoz, plural *kolkhozy*, was a form of collective farm in
the Soviet Union. In terms of Gulag and Gupvi camps, the
term *kolkhoz* was applied to any camp that was supposed to
provide agricultural products.

There is no barbed wire here. There are no fences at all, only
the dark forest pressing in around them, which is intimidating
enough. The prisoners are marched to their new living quarters, wooden cabins with tiny windows. Cilly steps inside her

new home. It is gloomy, with a single lonely light bulb dangling from the ceiling. In the middle of the room is a tall brick kiln, with bunk beds along the walls. In the middle of the camp, between the cabins, are two newer buildings: the kitchen and the hospital; both grey, single-storey wooden sheds. Unlike in Nizhny Tagil, there is no dedicated mess hall, just a small window in the kitchen building through which the daily rations are handed out to the prisoners. They can then either eat outside and fish mosquitoes and flies from their gruel in summer, or sit in the stinking gloom of their cabins in winter. There is no watchtower, only a large barracks for the guards in front of the camp. This camp is much smaller than the one they have been in before – just a *lagpunkt*, a branch of the main camp in nearby Sverdlovsk. It holds about 100 female prisoners, a quarter of the former camp. Cilly is happy that Angelika and the other women from her work brigade are still with her. After they move into their barracks, there is a roll call on the small square in front of the hospital. A man with a drooping moustache and dirty uniform steps in front of them. He has only one arm.

'Welcome! My name is Ivan Koltsov, and I am your brigadier. Here, you will cut trees in the woods and plant vegetables for the glorious Soviet Union under Comrade Stalin! Your guards will explain the details of our quota to you when you march to work tomorrow.'

'Not one of their quotas again!' Cilly whispers to Angelika and smiles.

'If you fulfil your daily quota you will live a good life here. We are not your enemies – if you work well you will be allowed to go home soon.'

The women stir and whisper as he speaks, but Cilly sees the three guards standing behind Ivan smile at each other, and her heart drops. Behind them in the forest, they can hear the trucks that brought them here rumble off, away into the darkness.

At the guards' barracks the next morning, the women are

handed tools. They are scheduled for wood cutting and receive new clothing to replace their torn Wehrmacht uniforms. The clothes make them look like the guards: long padded trousers, tied at the ankles, a long padded jacket and a fold-down fur hat with earflaps. The only items they do not receive are felt boots – instead they get rubber overshoes which they tie with wire or string to avoid losing them. There is no underwear, they just put the clothes over their naked skin. The jackets are stuffed into the trousers, in an attempt to cover the kidneys. And then the work begins: at six in the morning they are woken up, receive the usual 200 grams of bread and a quarter-litre of black tea. At seven they receive their tools – a dull pruning saw and a blunt axe. Then, under guard, they march into the forest. Emaciated and weak as they are, each prisoner is supposed to produce 2 cubic metres of wood daily – cut, loped off, sawed and stacked. They have to collect the branches and burn them. They cannot fulfil the quotas: just notching the trees with the blunt axe is wearing them down, and the trees are tall. It takes them a day just to fell one tree and cut off the branches. They try to use cut branches to lever the trees, but this is also a backbreaking task. The Russians mark the trees for each team, so there is enough space between work groups, but nevertheless there are still accidents and prisoners are maimed by falling timber. One day a tree falls in the wrong direction and crushes three prisoners to death. The women have to carry the bloody bodies to the small cemetery near the camp. When it gets too cold, the guards burn the branches; they are colder even than the women from standing around in the snow all day. The prisoners are allowed to warm up as well – their bodies cool down very quickly when they are not working. While warming up around the fire, sparks sometimes lodge in their padded clothing, and if the women do not pay attention they can continue to smoulder under the surface of the cloth. In the evening their faces are covered with soot. They all look like ogres – dirty, haggard, ragged – and move like old women. Their clothes constantly get stuck in the branches, and they can only wash with thawed snow in winter, if they have the time and energy, that is.

There are no veteran prisoners like Doris the cook here, and the women have to organise everything themselves: grave-digging and burials, cooking and cleaning. Angelika and two other women who have a talent for organisation soon become the camp elders and spokespeople, bargaining with Ivan for more food and better working hours. The other Russians, eight guards and a small wheezing doctor who spends his days in the hospital writing reports and smoking, have almost no interaction with the prisoners. They only shout '*Dawai!*' if it seems the women are not working fast enough. There is a small cell built under barracks number four, and Cilly wonders who it is for.

After a while she finds out. All the prisoners are suffering, and some of the young girls who have made it this far seem no longer able to take it – they go mad. One day at roll call, one 17-year-old woman named Ulrike suddenly runs to the gatehouse and shouts 'Let me out, my mother is outside, she's picking me up!' The guards fire some warning shots until she returns to the group and breaks down sobbing into the arms of her comrades. After that incident, Ulrike gets worse. Two weeks later, Cilly sees her incarcerated under barracks number four. She is sitting on dirty straw, her blonde hair dirty and in disarray, hugging herself and silently rocking back and forth. The guards push her daily bowl of *kasha* towards her with a broom handle. Sometimes she flings the food at the guards, sometimes she ignores it. After five days in the cell, Ulrike dies.

Over the summer of 1946, ten more women die in as many weeks, most of diseases like tuberculosis, brought on by malnutrition and their dirty surroundings. Ivan and the guards become afraid that they will be infected, and order Angelika and the others to set up containers with chlorinated water where the prisoners have to wash their plates, spoons and hands. They also force them to drink a green broth the doctor prepares – cooked pine needles, their daily vitamin C ration. The prisoners do not receive *kasha* without finishing their vitamins. In the outhouses the guards sprinkle a lot of chlorine.

Sometimes their brigade is transported to the edge of the forest by lorries, where there are fields up until the horizon, and the women have to skitter through weeds all day to harvest carrots, beetroots and cabbages. In Cilly's kolkhoz they also plant turnips, cucumbers and potatoes. When the weather is good they like to work in the fields, and during harvest time they can always eat some of the vegetables when the guards are not watching. After a while, they learn to crack sunflower seeds and spit out the husks as well as their Russian captors. Harvesting potatoes always reminds Cilly of her farm, of being out in the fields with her siblings, smiling despite the hard work. Her thoughts constantly circle around home, around what happened to her mother and Monika and the others now that the Russians are there, and she still hopes that she will be released soon. She will stay strong for her family.

Another task the women are given is to load the log barges that travel up and down a nearby river. The logs have been collected into large stacks by other work brigades, and the women from Ivan's camp have to roll them into the river to be collected as large rafts and pushed downriver by the barges. As they are supposed to start from the top of each stack, the women have to climb up, loosen the top log with crowbars and let it roll down into the river. One day it happens – the whole pile starts to move, and Cilly tumbles down with it. She is hurt so badly she can't even stand up. The logs have cut and bruised her legs and blood is running down into her boots. Nor can she sit down, so bruised is her behind. Together with a group of other sick and injured girls, the doctor sends her to a hut even deeper in the forest to recuperate. Cilly, in agony, thinks that they are stuck now, deserted like lepers. But after two days she mostly spends sleeping, she discovers that the short stay in the forest has its advantages: as most women in the group come from an agricultural background, they now have time to add whatever they find in the forest to their diet. They find large amounts of mushrooms and berries that they eat directly from the bushes or carry home for later, cowberries and raspberries they cook to make jam, with a sweet yellow berry they don't know the name of replacing sugar and gelatine. They also cook the mushrooms, which are delicious even without salt. The berries and mushrooms are welcome additions to their daily rations, which one of them has to fetch from the main camp. They receive dried produce – small fish that are crunchy with sand, and dry bread. In that hut Cilly recovers a little, despite the feeling of abandonment and her constant pain. Shortly before they return to the main camp, one of the girls gets lost in the woods while gathering berries and only returns after three days – she is found by the guards and returned to the camp. The other women do not recognise her, as her face and extremities are swollen from mosquito bites.

The next day they learn something extraordinary: even here, near this godforsaken kolkhoz, there is a bathhouse. From the outside it looks like a wooden hut, and inside are troughs filled with steaming hot water. Everyone wants to be the first to wash, as even the second person has to wash with pretty cloudy water. At two other tubs they are allowed to wash their hair, and a Russian woman employed by the guards sets a bucket with ash next to the tubs, indicating for them to use it as shampoo.

'What? She must be mad!' Angelika says, running through the ash with her fingers.

'At least we can try it,' Cilly says. 'The Russians must be using it, so it can't be that bad.'

She wets her hair, takes a handful of ash and rubs it in. It is not unpleasant, and even foams a bit. The other women also use the ash, and laughing and fooling around they finish their toilet. They receive their clothes back, which had been sent to be deloused in the meantime, and are sent back to camp. After a while Cilly realises that her hair has become quite soft and feels good, all through the use of the ash it seems.

Summer 1947. The work and exertions are the same as before, but the situation with their guards has improved somewhat. Ivan the camp commander is quiet and friendly – and most importantly, he does not bully them like the other guards, maybe because he never has to venture out with them and instead drives a small horse-drawn cart over to the main camp in Sverdlovsk to get supplies when the guards and prisoners are out in the fields. Maybe his friendliness is due to his affair with Bettina, a tall blonde prisoner, who starts to spend nights with him in his room in the guard barracks. It is a bit strange for the other women at first, but they also benefit somewhat when Bettina brings extra food from the guards' table and shares it with the comrades in her barracks.

Before the supply situation started to improve in late 1947 and early 1948, few of the malnourished and weak women had thought of physical intimacies – work, hunger and exhaustion dominated everything. Later, there were affairs between guards and inmates, or among inmates in mixed camps. In Gulag camps for Soviet citizens there were also love affairs between inmates of the same sex, and the same is likely in the all-female German Gupvi camps. Cilly never spoke about any aspect of this, but it existed.

One day in 1947 the prisoners are sent to receive new clothes. After two years of working in the forest, in the fields and building roads, the women still wear the dirty and torn camp uniforms. But when they see what they are supposed to wear, they are shocked. Piled on the floor is a big heap of wrinkled and soiled Red Army clothing, dirty brown trousers and shirts. Some have large blood stains, others bullet holes.

'We will never wear that! They can wear it themselves!'

Everyone is shouting, and Cilly remembers when they received uniform items two years back – it seems the Russians have run out of Wehrmacht clothing. Angelika walks over to

Cilly with an oil-stained pair of brown trousers.

'If at least we could wash these things …'

There is no running water in the camp, and they are not allowed to wash clothes in the bathhouse. In the end, most women decide to wear the clothing, so on the next day at roll call there is a completely new sight – rows of women in too-large Red Army uniform pieces standing to attention, like a group of schoolchildren who have plundered the wardrobe of their older siblings. If they had shaved heads and machine guns they would look like proper Red Army soldiers, Cilly thinks. But she wonders what the women would do if someone handed them guns at this very moment, and looks at the guards.

Then she is put to work in a bog. With pointy shovels the prisoners cut square pieces of peat from the bog, and other workers put these up in pyramid-shaped heaps for drying. Summers here are hot, very hot. The sun burns down on the prisoners toiling in the bog, they are tormented by midges and their stomachs still rumble all the time. When Ivan is not in sight, the guards constantly harass and rush the women to fulfil their quotas, so there are no real breaks. Cilly's fingers and hands are covered in blisters and she is always tired.

One morning she wakes up with a fever. At first she pushes herself to work, but the fever does not abate after a week, and as she feels worse than after her earlier injury, Angelika sends her to the hospital.

'The doctor won't kill you – and you can always say that you feel better and come back to work. He might even send you back to the huts in the forest and you can bring us some berries!'

She is right – most women who reported sick have either been sent to the hut in the woods to recover or returned to work after a few days in the hospital. So the next morning Cilly reports sick and walks over to the infirmary. The camp doctor takes her temperature, listens to her breathing and sticks a piece of wood down her throat.

'Pneumonia! This just means that you can no longer work in the fields. You have to stay here until you get better. Take the top bunk in the next room!'

So she is allowed time off work again, this time not in the deserted hut in the forest but in a small room in the infirmary where she is the only patient. There are three rooms with two bunk beds per room, with soft sheets and a woollen blanket. This is the first bed linen Cilly has seen in two years. She also receives a large piece of fragrant soap. There are no bugs here and there's even a toilet in the hallway, so she does not have to use the outhouse. However, Cilly still only staggers to the toilet and washroom, and back to her bed, that's how weak she is. There are no drugs in the hospital, and wounds are dressed with toilet paper – too rare to use for its intended purpose. Even old newspapers are rare, as the smokers use them to roll cigarettes. Cilly is in the hospital for weeks. Each morning, de-spite her raging fever and a dizziness that is getting worse and worse, she has to report to the doctor for a check-up. After-wards she receives her breakfast, wolfs it down and just sinks back into her bunk. But she cannot sleep properly, thrashing around her bunk with a pain in her lower back that keeps get-ting worse and worse. It hurts when she has to pee, and there is blood in her urine.

The doctor can't really help – the only medication he offers is some sort of yellowish powder, a generic heal-all for all sorts of sicknesses, which he sprinkles over rashes and cuts and uses to make a chest wrap for Cilly. She also receives her daily ration of the 'vitamin broth' made from pine needles. Nothing im-proves her condition.

Cilly did not have pneumonia. After the war, a doctor spe-cialising in the treatment of former POWs will tell her what she was suffering from: tuberculosis of the kidneys. Tubercu-losis is a common, and in many cases fatal, infectious disease caused by mycobacteria that dwell in unhygienic surroundings. Tuberculosis typically attacks the lungs, but can also affect other parts of the body. About one in ten latent infections eventually progresses to become the active disease which, if left untreated, kills more than half of those infected. It is a disease born out of dirt and a weak immune system, and it killed many women in the camps.

Diagnosis of tuberculosis relies on radiology, commonly chest X-rays, as well as microscopic examination. Treatment is difficult and requires administration of multiple antibiotics over a long period of time. Of course, none of this is available in the camp in the forest in 1947. Cilly's diagnosis would have been urogenital tuberculosis, had anyone diagnosed her. For the moment, as with a variety of sicknesses the camp doctor lacks the means to diagnose, it's pneumonia. After she returned to Germany, she had to go to a specialist clinic three times to address the long-term effects of her sickness.

~

I wonder what she thought and did when she realised that this was more serious than all that had gone before. Did she realise that the pain in her back and groin meant that something serious was advancing on her? And how did she emerge from it? Maybe she prayed or thought of home, her salvation, and then with all her focus and strength she must have pushed the pain and sickness away from her mind, forced down the dizziness and cramps and aches. That's what I would do — focus on the daily routine, and if there is none in the wooden shed where they keep you, create one. Get up early, eat all the food they give you, force yourself to walk around the room for two hours, then sit down and wait for lunch. Sleep as much as possible. I still cannot imagine it, being sick for weeks in a row and not succumbing, not letting the sickness run its course and finish you off, not following all the other emaciated and hungry women who had taken the one escape available to them.

I don't understand how Cilly survived this. No one was able to treat her symptoms beyond sprinkling her with yellow powder and giving her pine needle broth, but she survived. She was in pain all the time. I can barely imagine the strength of will it must have taken to push the pain into a part of her mind where it did not impair her ability to work, so they would give her full rations. Maybe she drank a lot of water and flushed out her kidneys, or perhaps it was pure luck. Or beneath the surface of the jolly round grandmother that I knew and loved, there was a hard and strong woman. Or perhaps, by the time I knew her, that woman had gone. Maybe Cilly had left her behind, out in the forests near Revda in the Sverdlovskaya Oblast.

In the end, whenever she talked about her sickness – and she rarely said anything other than that she had been sick and nearly died – she ascribed her survival to food, again. After the infirmary, when she had recovered somewhat, they put her in the kitchen.

~

Together with five other women she is ordered to work here – and that is a good thing. They have to scrub the soup and *kasha* cauldrons, and that way they always have enough to eat. This is a privilege that really surprises her, and she wonders if Bettina and Angelika have influenced Ivan in some way. In the kitchen she finds out where Ivan got his impressive belly. Once, through the half-open door to the larder, she spots a block of butter, easily 25 or 30 kilograms. Also sides of bacon, white as snow, corned beef and large sugar loafs. Cilly thinks these products are all meant for the prisoners, but it is Ivan and the guards who take them from the larder and eat them in their barracks. Her daily routine is as follows: washing the steel plates, cutting dried salted fish, making a fire, cooking *kasha*.

Making a fire isn't that easy. They only have freshly cut wood, still green, and birch bark as firelighters – matches are rare. But they always manage to make a fire, sometimes it just takes a while to get started. Sometimes it happens that the soup isn't properly cooked by the time the other women return from work in the evening, but it is still dished out.

One day a committee of Red Cross doctors visits, a farce performed by the Soviets to give the impression that the prisoners are treated well. Cilly and the other women are allowed to use real flour to bake white bread; bacon is added to the *kasha* and the soup, and the yard is raked and laid out with white pebbles and flower beds for the three doctors and their NKVD guide to strut around. They nod approvingly and take notes on a clipboard. Once the committee is gone, so is the good food. The committee visits once a year, but the doctors never speak to the prisoners to learn anything about life in the kolkhoz. And everywhere around them, in camps all over the Soviet Union, people are still starving to death. For Cilly, the most important part of kitchen work is that she can finally eat her fill. She polishes off her bread ration of 500 grams, three bowls of cabbage soup and even some leftovers from the guards' rooms when collecting dishes there. But she has been hungry so long, it seems as if she can no longer sate her appetite – she is still hungry.

One day they run out of cabbage, and have only groats left to make *kasha* for 100 people – the soup is thin. Together with the dried and salted fish, this is not a delicacy. Some of the women bring nettles with them from the woods, and they decide to try to cook nettle soup. The doctor and Ivan really like the idea, so every day they send out a group of women (guarded, of course) to collect nettles. From then on the menu is: nettle soup in the morning, nettle soup followed by groat *kasha* at midday and nettle soup with salt fish in the evening.

After a few months in the kitchen Cilly feels a little better, so she is scheduled to work in the 'bog brigade' again. Now their work is mowing swamp grass. They stand in the bog up to their knees, plagued by midges and flies. Ivan has measured out their work area and marked it with sticks, and again they are given a quota, and again they cannot fulfil it. But one day when they return from the bog, filthy and tired, there is a letter waiting for her.

10 THE ROAD IS A GREY TAPE

I have the most evil memories of Spain, but I have very few bad memories of Spaniards.

George Orwell, *Homage to Catalonia*

I'm sitting in a restaurant with at least 500 seats, large windows which look out on a leafy avenue, and a complete fire engine in the middle of the room, serving as the bar. It's early evening, and besides a loud and raucous dinner party some tables down from me, I'm the only guest. Three young waiters with cropped blond hair stare at me as I fumble with the menu, and I feel relieved when Luba arrives. Luba Suslyakova is a slender, impish-looking woman with a broad smile who works as a tour guide and blogger of Lonely Planet fame, and she has agreed to help me visit Cilly's former camps. We sit down and finally one of the waiters can take our orders.

After discussing my travel plans for the next days, I ask Luba why there seems to be no real nightlife culture in Russia.

'You have to understand that this is something we are just learning. In Communist times people were just not going out, for example with their co-workers, as they were afraid they might say something wrong when drunk and get arrested the next day.'

Most restaurants and bars are either franchised Irish, English or Scottish pubs or strange themed restaurants like the firefighter restaurant we are sitting in, or the cheap German restaurant on the main square I visited a few days earlier. There are no Communist hospitality leftovers like Poland's vodka

and beer bars here, which I point out to Luba. 'Today, as drinking vodka is always linked with eating here, even if it's only a
few snacks accompanying the shots, most nightclubs offer
proper food throughout the night. So you can feast on dumplings and chicken with mashed potatoes at four in the morning, if you like,' she says.

'But what did people do when they can't go to nightclubs?
There must have been the urge to celebrate and relax with a
few friends, surely?' I ask.

'Yes – in the kitchen. What would happen is that you would
buy a few bottles of vodka on the way home, invite your friends
and then all gather in the kitchen. That was the Russian safe
place.'

On cue, our food arrives, and I tell her about my hotel, the
former KGB headquarters, and mention that I have had problems sleeping in the last few days. While I put this down to my
financial problems and belated train-jetlag, Luba has another
theory.

'People around here say that all guests staying in your hotel
either cannot sleep or have nightmares all the time,' she says,
'because of all the people they shot in the basement.'

I almost choke on my sandwich.

The death toll from the Great Terror of 1936 to 1938 – Stalin's purges of enemies, real and imagined – was 700,000, and
historians estimate the total number of victims of his political
repressions at anywhere between 3 million and 39 million. In
Yekaterinburg alone, there is a mass grave of 30,000 victims.
Some were shot after the NKVD brought them to their headquarters and extorted a confession. To this day, more and
more mass graves from the 1930s are being discovered around
the city. Communists and Nazis, terror and terror. I cannot
finish my sandwich. Let's get back to Cilly, and her hope, and
her letter.

In *Im Archipel GUPVI*, Stefan Karner writes:

From spring 1946, POWs in the Soviet Union were allowed to send Red Cross postcards home [...] The cards, which the prisoners sent home from the camps, already contained a small response card. This enabled the prisoners to receive word from home.

~

Cilly had been allowed to write a card home to the farm when the Red Cross visited the forest camp for the first time, but she never hoped to receive anything back. What happened to her mother and her little sister, now that she was gone? Did the Russians leave them in peace? Or was Monika taken as well, lost in another dreadful camp? The postcard she was allowed to send was limited to 25 words, which would certainly have been censored as well – so she only transmitted the most basic information, not open to any interpretation.

Mir geht es gut, ich habe Arbeiten und bin gesund. Bin in Russland und hoffe bald nach Hause zu kommen. Wo seid ihr jetzt?

I am well, I have work and am healthy. Am in Russia and hope to return home soon. Where are you now?

The correspondences between Cilly and home do not survive, so I have made them up, these words. What can you write with 25 words to the people you love, who may not be alive, whom you may never find again?

But they live, and when Cilly returns from her work in the bog she is elated to find Ivan handing them the return slips from their postcards. Some immediately lie down on their bunks to read their cards, others hide them in their tunics and go for food first, saving the letter from their loved ones to be savoured as the sweetest of desserts. Cilly does the same and, after wolfing down her *kasha* and slice of bread, hurries to her barracks to find out who has written to her, and with what news.

It's a letter from her mother, a small postcard with 25 new words for her on it, another 25 words I have made up.

Bin auf dem Hof deiner Schwester Lucie, Moni bei Otti. Uns geht es gut, Hof zerstört. Komm nicht hier her. Schreib Familie Maus in Solingen.

I am on the farm of your sister Lucie, Monika with Otti. We are well, farm destroyed. Don't come here. Write to family Maus in Solingen.

Cilly is so happy and confused she can hardly focus on her mother's tiny handwriting, and reads the card over and over again. So her mother is with her older sister Lucie, on the farm owned by Lucie's husband Franz, and Monika is in Allenstein with her half-sister Otti. But what is this about the farm being destroyed? And why family Maus in Solingen?

~

The destruction of the family homestead is shrouded in mystery. Some say it was reoccupied and destroyed by the Wehrmacht in a final and forlorn push for Allenstein, some say it was the Red Army that burned it to the ground by accident. I never found out what happened – the building vanished from the land, like most of my family.

After the war ended, Cilly was in Russia, her mother and sister with their relatives, but there was already pressure on the German citizens remaining in East Prussia from the Polish authorities, which, since mid-1945, had occupied and administered this area of the former German Reich. At the Potsdam Conference in July 1945, the territory east of the Oder–Neisse line was assigned to Polish and Soviet Union administration. All Germans had their property confiscated and were placed under restrictive jurisdiction, and all property, abandoned or not, was declared to belong to the Polish People's Republic.

Around the same time, Stalin started shifting people around again: 5 million Germans resided east of the Oder–

Neisse line. By the beginning of 1946, 550,000 Germans had been expelled. In February 1946, 2,288,000 persons were classified as Germans, and those who could not demonstrate their 'Polish nationality' were directed for expulsion. But as most of my family spoke Polish, and at least half of the family had sympathised with the Polish cause, they were allowed to stay in the new Polish territories. But nevertheless, they advised Cilly not to come back, and go instead to a family named Maus, who had been regular summer guests of the family on the farm and to whom Otto had business connections for farm produce. They lived in a small town in the west of Germany: Solingen.

~

A week later, Cilly is allowed to accompany Ivan to the main camp to get provisions, as she has developed another large blister on her left foot and the doctor in the camp is busy with other patients. They drive to the main camp in his small cart. Cilly tries to explain to Ivan that it is called a *Panjewagen* in German, but he only smiles and nods. They arrive at the main camp after two hours. This is the main administrative camp for the Sverdlovsk region. The size is comparable to her camp in Nizhny Tagil, but there is a proper hospital with an elderly Russian doctor in charge who seems quite competent and trustworthy. There are also nurses in tidy white uniforms from Hungary, prisoners themselves, who appear to Cilly like creatures from another planet. These are the first female prisoners not being used for physical labour that she has seen in almost two years. The wooden barracks are like something from a lost world, resembling proper houses, some even with two storeys and colourful carved balustrades. There is a large administrative building with an attached storeroom where Ivan stops and tells her to wait for him. Cilly can study the other inmates, and wonders whether it was fate or the Lord who stuck her out in the woods. In the camp, the displaced women from Romania and Hungary still wear their traditional costumes and do not look like downtrodden slaves who stumble around the compound looking at their feet, but instead smile and wave at each other and have time to stop and engage in chit-chat. Cilly is stunned and at the same time reminded of East Prussia, where some of the neighbouring farmer families also wore colourful folk dresses in summer, especially for big festivals. She swallows her tears and hobbles to the hospital to have her blister looked after.

In the large and surprisingly clean hospital, the bespectacled and friendly-looking doctor sets to work and opens the blister over a kidney basin. Cilly does not even flinch, and afterwards he applies a dressing, which enables her to walk properly again. She is almost outside the hospital already when she gathers her strength and goes back.

The doctor looks up as she enters the room again.

'I am really sorry, but I wonder if it is possible to get transferred to the main camp here? I am strong and a good cook – I work in the kitchen in the forest!'

The doctor takes off his glasses and looks at her, with her dirty and torn padded jacket, her headscarf askew and a dressing around her left foot. He hesitates a moment, and then shakes his head.

'You must return to the kolkhoz for the time being, everything else will be seen to. I will take note and ask the camp commander here.'

He then proceeds to scribble something on a piece of paper and shakes Cilly's hand. She leaves the hospital in excellent spirits and smiles at Ivan as she clambers on board the cart. This elation, however, does not last long, as she never hears anything from the doctor in the main camp.

Back in the forest camp, Cilly is ordered by Ivan to leave her workplace in the kitchen and to make space for another woman returning to work from the infirmary, who also needs all the food she can get. Cilly is not angry at Ivan, and instructs her replacement before joining her comrades again. Angelika smiles at her as they march out of the camp and falls in next to her.

This time, the brigade is marched north for two hours and then they have to row across a large lake in small boats. When they reach the other side there's a shed where three guards and a few horses are stationed, and together with the animals the women are supposed to fetch logs from the forest, which are then bundled onto rafts on the lake. Cilly wonders what will happen with all the wood as there seems to be no river large enough to take all the logs away, but she has long stopped questioning seemingly illogical work orders in this world of quotas, one-, and five- and ten-year plans.

It has become very hot. Horseflies and mosquitoes torment the horses and the women all day, especially when the sun is highest up in the sky. Between noon and 2 p.m. they cannot work at all, hiding in their jackets folded over their heads and plugging the buttonholes with pieces of wood. Over their heads, swarms of mosquitoes swoosh around like attacking fighter planes. In the evenings they return to camp across the lake, the little boat, which only holds five prisoners and a guard, going back and forth until the whole brigade has reached the shore.

One cannot live in captivity for four years in different places in one country and not see beauty, at least specks of it, despite being a prisoner of war and longing for home. Perhaps Cilly found aspects of that beauty here, after recovering from her sickness and receiving word from home, after regaining hope. She glides across a lake, not unlike the ones at home, the water very quiet and the setting sun glittering on the water and amongst the trees on the shoreline; as the other prisoners sink the paddles in and small waves lap against the boat. Sometimes a large bird of prey will start circling over the lake, or a flock of sparrows flaps low over the water from one side to the other. It is unreal to Cilly, yet still she is in the midst of this beauty.

In the woods and beyond the woods, over the mountains and on the plains of the north and in the factories and cities and building sites in Moscow and on the Volga, there are the camps where women and men are still dying in droves. But here on the lake there is peace. Between one shore and the other, they are safe, suspended in time. There are five women in the boat from all over Europe and all have survived to this point. There is no sense of joy or thankfulness in my grandmother out on the lake, but a moment of release and peace.

A few days later, the women are marched to a new area of the forest to cut trees, and discover wooden barracks standing in a clearing. These are inhabited by young mothers with little children, ten or 20 small families without men. The women speak German and identify themselves as Volga Germans from the area around Saratow, and tell a story that even the German women from Cilly's camp find hard to comprehend. They had been woken up in the dead of night and separated from their husbands, who were herded onto waiting trucks while the women and children were allowed 15 minutes to pack their most important belongings and then marched to the train station. There, they had to surrender the remainder of their luggage, were pushed into cattle wagons and transported here, where they were abandoned in the middle of nowhere with no instructions or news. Like the inhabitants of the sick barracks in the woods, they live on what they can forage from the forest. They do not know where their husbands are. Cilly is witnessing another aspect of Soviet resettlement efforts, still in place long after the war had ended.

~

Stalin liked to move people around the Soviet Union like peas on a plate. During and after World War II, the Soviet government conducted a series of mass deportations, displacing around 1.9 million people to Siberia and the Central Asian Soviet republics. Collaboration with the Germans and anti-Soviet factions were the official reasons for these deportations. Volga Germans were just one nationality deported: Crimean Tatars, Kalmyks, Chechens, Ingush, Balkars, Karachays, Meskhetian Turks, Bulgarians, Crimean Greeks, Romanians and Armenians were also 'resettled'. In May 1944, all Crimean Tatars were deported to the Uzbek Soviet Socialist Republic as a form of collective punishment. Nearly 20 per cent of them died in exile during the following year and a half. Poland and Soviet Ukraine also conducted population exchanges – the 'Flight and Expulsion' of the Poles that I learned about back in Olsztyn. Around 2.1 million Poles who resided east of the new Poland–Russia border were deported to Poland, and around 450,000 Ukrainians on the other side of the border were deported to Soviet Ukraine between September 1944 and April 1946.

I again wonder what all these forced migrations meant to Soviet society and family, and if there is a sense of place and home prevailing in modern Russian society today. Luba has invited me to the regular meet-up of the local English club, an informal gathering of locals who get together to converse and improve their English on a weekly basis. Luba is one of the founders, so she has invited me to come along and talk about my trip and Cilly. In the afternoon, I arrive at yet another restaurant. This time it's in the basement and has a traditional Russian theme, with colourful tapestries on the wall and dark wooden furniture. I'm ushered by the long-legged waitress to a smaller private room, where a friendly group of Russians and a few expats living in Yekaterinburg are expecting me. The setting is cosy, with sofas and more traditional tapestry on the wall. Everyone is very polite and smiling and they have Guinness on the menu, so after a drink and a quick introduction I set off, telling the story of my trip and Cilly's, handing around copies of her NKVD file and the few maps I have. I then ask what people think about the forced migration and its impact on society.

'No one is from anywhere in Russia,' says Yulia, a pretty blonde woman sitting next to me.

'My family is from Lviv in the Ukraine, but my father was sent here to work so he raised the family in Yekaterinburg. Most people here in the room have family elsewhere, and are the first or second generation living in the city.'

It transpires that the grandparents or parents of most young people here came voluntarily or were sent here to work for the arms industries: there are people from Lviv, Moscow, St Petersburg, the Crimea. And while not all of them have seen an NKVD/KGB file before, the fact that so many people from all over the Soviet Union and Europe landed here does not raise an eyebrow.

'Up until the 1990s, Yekaterinburg was part of the "forbidden zone" of the Urals, an area of industry and weapons production for the Red Army,' Luba tells me, 'and only special workers were allowed to come here and travel through the region.'

We continue to chat, and Luba tells the story of how she visited one of the prisons in the area with one of her tour clients, and that the first thing she encountered was a large painting of Stalin inside. The influence of 'Uncle Joe', as the Americans called Stalin during the war, and the impact of his camps still loom large in certain parts of Russia.

I want to find out more about the labour history of Yekaterinburg though, so the next day I take the metro to travel north of the city centre. Emerging on a small square in what looks like a housing estate bordered by a busy commuter road, I meet Dmitry and Sasha. The two young journalists in their twenties run the 'Tesnota' Webzine, and have offered me a tour of the so-called Uralmash area. Both would not look out of place in Berlin Kreuzberg: Dmitry is tall with a shaved head, earrings and a striped jumper, and Sasha has a mass of unruly black hair and wears thick-rimmed glasses. He proudly shows me a vin-

15   Postcard of Uralmash, 1965

tage analogue camera.

'This is a very famous Soviet product, the "Vigilant" camera,' Sasha says.

'We would like to take some pictures of you walking around Uralmash, I hope that is all right!'

Uralmash is an abbreviation of *Uralskiie Mashinostroitelnyy Zavod*, Urals Machine-Building Plant. Today, it is a heavy machine production facility owned by the Russian engineering corporation OMZ, and also gives its name to the surrounding residential area where the workers live.

'This is a proper piece of Yekaterinburg history here,' Dmitry tells me.

'The factory began operations in 1933 and manufactured products for the mining and metallurgical industries in the Urals and Siberia. During World War II they produced T-34 tanks and SU-100 gun tank destroyers here.'

We walk into the red dusk of city summer, with the sun tinting the clouds above the prefabricated high-rise apartments across the road pink and brown. Exhaust fumes and the smell of wet asphalt are in the air, as someone has just watered the plants near the entrance to the station. I'm surprised: I was expecting more 1980s concrete and plastic, but the Uralmash buildings are red brick from the 1950s, with streets lined with trees and parks, and a series of interconnected courtyards.

As we walk, Dmitry keeps lining out the history of Uralmash.

'After World War II, the state made large investments in the reconstruction and expansion of the factory and workers' quarter, which is what you see here today. This favoured output and the production of new machines and equipment – shovels, drilling rigs, crushers and mills. Uralmash actually produced the drill for the Kola superdeep borehole project, which attempted to drill as deep as possible into the Earth's crust in 1970 and is still the deepest borehole on the planet. The factory is still in operation and is one of the main employers in the area today.'

We walk past parked cars, lattice fences covered in bleached-out posters, and dogs trotting around the courtyards, unfazed by the clusters of men sitting on plastic chairs, chatting. Sasha keeps snapping away and sometimes positions me in dark alleyways or in front of boarded-up houses. I tell Sasha and Dmitry that this area would be prime gentrification material in Berlin.

'Not here!' Sasha laughs while rewinding the film in his camera.

'It is still mainly used by the workers. And some are working on top-secret armament projects these days. There are even urban myths connected with the area and the factory: to this day, inhabitants swear they hear strange noises underground, like heavy equipment being moved and subway trains going back and forth, even though the metro line of Yekaterinburg runs miles further to the south.'

Again, there seems to be something hidden behind the facade in Russia, but no one knows where the myths come from. As it gets dark, we walk back to the metro station, past vodka-drinking bums under plastic pavilions.

'But maybe there is a grain of truth to the story of the secret Uralmash metro,' Dmitry says.

'Sasha and I were visiting Moscow a few years back, and we met a drunk man who claimed to be a metro driver. He told us that he worked on the secret metro line that links the Kremlin with Stalin's former dacha, his weekend home in the suburbs. The jobs on these lines were officially offered to metro drivers on the regular Moscow metro, he told us. The pay was much better, but the working hours were long and he had to sign a special contract that forbade him to speak about the metro and whom he transported. Maybe he really was a bum, but something clicked when we heard his story ...'

I say goodbye to Dmitry and Sasha at the metro station and walk back to my hotel, the former KGB headquarters. Layers and layers of history around me, I think.

A few days later, the two email me the pictures, which have turned out as expected: most are either over- or underexposed; a few show bits and pieces of me, a hat, half a face, one side of my T-shirt, wrapped in darkness, wrinkles. There is one image that I particularly like, a dark silhouette of me visible in the entrance to a courtyard. It feels like an adequate representation

16 Marcel in Uralmash

of how I feel looking for Cilly. Half there, half here, and everything wrapped in shadows.

~

In Cilly's woods, the days get colder and shorter, and one day
it suddenly starts to snow. Again, they have to go to the latrine
trenches in the dark, always in twos, as the wolves are howling
in the woods. It is frightening. Their guards tell them to be
watchful: if they see something shining in the night, shining
like small torches, it is the eyes of wolves.

In the spring of 1948, Ivan announces that all good workers,
which includes Cilly, will receive a ten-day break. The prisoners think it's a joke, but then the guards really do set up an additional room in the infirmary, with five bunk beds with straw
mattresses, a table and a bench. In rotation, for ten days each,
five women are allowed to rest there, without work and on full
rations. They are allowed to sleep as long as they want, and no
one calls them out to morning roll call. On Sundays the prisoners are even allowed to go to the forest and search for strawberries, raspberries and mushrooms. For Cilly's short time
there, she can breathe more freely, and during their Sunday
excursion she is able to stuff her mouth with raspberries and
even to nap in a clearing, falling asleep with the sun on her face.

After her break, Cilly has to go back to work. She is sent to
join a team working on the roads in a nearby village, and here
the work is even harder than the field and river work before, as
if to make up for the rest days. The prisoners have to cart heavy
stones around, break them up with iron hammers, carry sand
from lorries to the building site, and then set the stones down
on the street and hammer them down to make a smooth surface. And this time they are also unlucky with the guards –
these new fellows are really harsh, pushing them around and
refusing them breaks. They are often dizzy from hunger and
tiredness, and from May onwards the sun is scorching. By

June, they are working right in the middle of a small town nearby, and here Cilly witnesses for the first time that not all Russians consider her a fascist prisoner; to some she is a fellow human being. Sometimes, when most of the guards are on lunchbreak and only one post watches over them, a Russian granny or an old man walks over to where the prisoners are working and presses a piece of bread or some boiled potatoes into their hands. The first time it happens, Cilly is perplexed, almost shocked. Judging from the shabby surroundings on the main street and the state of the wooden buildings lining it, townspeople are poor themselves, but most are warm-hearted and helpful. Their new guards, however, are not: once, one of them sees such an exchange, walks over and demands the bread for himself. One day, Cilly, stooped over and crushing stones, is suddenly handed a 20-rouble note. Without thinking she snatches it, and before she can straighten up and have a good look, her benefactor has already hobbled away – she sees only the hunched back of a Russian babushka. The guard has not seen anything, so she suddenly has 20 roubles and can buy a few *bulkis*, rolls, for the comrades and herself in a nearby bakery.

In *Im Archipel GUPVI*, Stefan Karner writes:

In strong contrast to the propaganda image of the Soviet enemy are the many positive and engaged recollections of former POWs, especially about the life and meaning of the Russian women for family and society and about the 'common Russian'. A shared portion of porridge, the offer of a cigarette or another sacrificing gesture remained strongly in their memories and presented a new picture of 'the Russian', who often – even in situations when he had almost nothing left to survive – shared what he had.

By now, after almost four years in Russia, most prisoners have snatched up enough Russian words to have a basic conversation, and now that they are again working in more urban surroundings after years in the forest there is more potential for interaction with the outside world. And Cilly finds out that there is a black market. So one day she decides to participate herself. She has traded a woollen jacket with nice brass buttons from one of the Volga German women for a knife stolen from the tool shed, so she first sells the eight buttons on the jacket, which buys her a bottle of milk and a piece of bread spread thickly with butter. That isn't much, but the milk and butter do her good. The following week, she sells the whole jacket for another bottle of milk, a pat of butter and a bucket full of potatoes. The only question is how to get the food into camp: at the gate they are always searched by the guards when returning from town. Usually, a tall, blonde 18-year-old German male prisoner from a nearby camp, employed by the guards, waits for them at the gate. The women call him the 'hound', because he is very good at sniffing out contraband and lets nothing pass – he is even more ruthless and eager than the guards. They drink the milk on the spot; Cilly hides the butter against her chest and Angelika and the other women share the potatoes out, secreting them in their boots and the hems of their long work trousers. Then they march to the camp gate – and sigh with relief. The 'hound' isn't working.

In December 1948, Cilly's improved Russian language skills help her. She is still building roads in the same small town as before, and when the man operating the concrete mixer becomes ill, the construction site brigadier asks if someone knows how to work the thing, and Cilly raises her hand without hesitation. She picks up how to work the machine quickly – she has to – and from then on she has to be at the site before the others to prepare the concrete, mixing the right proportions of limes and sand with water. For that she receives a special *propusk* – a pass that allows her to leave the camp alone. This is a huge privilege. Now, she can just walk around and polish up her Russian, bartering with the locals whenever she or one of the other prisoners has something to barter with.

Most mornings when she is alone at the construction site, Cilly is able to barter with an elderly woman who lives nearby: she brings her some firewood from the site and receives leftover food in exchange.

Close to the construction site there is a prison. One day shortly before Christmas, while she is standing by her concrete mixer and slapping her arms against the frost that has invaded the Urals again, a young man walks over to her with his two small children, a boy on his arm and a thin girl clinging to his leg, their noses running in the cold. He is waiting for visiting hours at the prison so he can see his wife, and they start to talk. He tells her that his wife had been mobilised to work at a nearby kolkhoz for 70 days, while he was away fighting in the war. When his wife learned that he had returned home, she left the kolkhoz three days before her allotted 70 days were over. And for this she has now been imprisoned. Cilly is shocked – the husband returns after years in war, and his wife is jailed for the most natural and understandable impulse.

The new year arrives, after a somewhat uplifting Christmas with enough food and carols sung around the stoves in the barracks. This year, 1949, will be her last in the Soviet Union, but she does not know this yet. Instead, the women again return to cutting trees in the forest. In April, however, their situation improves. Cilly, Angelika and the others from the brigade are moved again, this time to Revda. This is an industrial camp in one of the factory cities that were built during the war, again with barbed wire, guard towers and shifts at factories. But when they are transported away from their now empty camp in the woods in trucks again, no one looks back or even wonders what is happening to them. After four years, they have all become veterans of the camp, and being moved to a new place of work without any notice is nothing new to them. The situation in the new camp is better. The camp is divided into two sections – one for men and one for women, with a fence in the middle. Around the whole camp there is again a double barbed wire fence. On the men's side there is the *banja*, the bathhouse, and the kitchen as well as the hospital, which the women can only visit in groups and with the permission of the guards. During the first weeks it is strictly forbidden to talk with the men.

Political re-education is on the menu now. Some German officials from the so-called Antifa, the counter-fascism group set up by the Soviet government, come to their camp and give talks about how the war started, who started it and why the prisoners should abandon fascism. Sometimes they also show movies. That's nice. Otherwise it is just praising Stalin, and long lectures about the Communist Party of the Soviet Union. The prisoners have to learn Communist 'facts' by heart, and the prisoners, including Cilly, are taught to write using the Cyrillic alphabet. The courses are not voluntary: the Antifa teachers say the prisoners have to receive a certain mark, otherwise they will not be allowed to return home. Cilly does not like the political classes in the camp; she is just waiting to go home. She has exchanged more letters with her family, and her mind is made up: she will not return to East Prussia immediately but try her luck with family Maus in Solingen first.

The food is much better in Revda too: there is coffee instead of water in the morning, and every single day there is a spoonful of sugar and a piece of fish. Once a week they receive some tobacco. This is where Cilly picks up smoking: when the women first receive the tobacco, they barter with male prisoners crossing over to their side of the camp to hand in their sugar and receive tobacco in exchange. One of the men shows Cilly how to roll and pinch a cigarette out of newspaper like the Russians, and after a few tries and heavy coughing, she starts to like the slightly numbing effect the cigarettes have on her tongue and mind. Her work brigade is assigned to the town's stone and clay factory and has to do some heavy lifting and carrying for a few weeks. Then she is moved to a new workplace nearby. As usual, the prisoners gather at the gate in the morning and are then led to a pit near the camp. Each woman is given a shovel and has to lay the groundwork for railroad tracks under the watchful eye of a Ukrainian foreman. The work is hard, but they are no longer the weak and shivering emaciated women who were brought to Russia in 1945, not knowing what would happen to them. By now most of them speak Russian with the guards to demand water or breaks, and they joke with each other in German while pounding away with the shovels at the dirty ground. They have a 1.5-hour lunchbreak and return to the camp to eat.

Later, the female prisoners are allowed to have contact with the male camp. There is a soldier named Jürgen who used to work for the theatre in Hamburg, who organises 'colourful evenings'. He writes poems and sketches for the others to perform, using pieces of wood for notes that he 'inscribes' with pieces of broken glass and scrubs clean with the same glass after. Something like a cultural life starts in the camp – the women's camp form a choir, where Cilly and Angelika sing and Angelika even conducts the singers. The male prisoners do the same. They have a brilliant soloist – a carpenter. One evening, both choirs perform together in the large main hall of the hospital, accompanied by a prisoner who plays an old battered guitar. Their audience are sick and healthy prisoners, as well as the Russian guards. Cilly and the others stand at the front of the warm room, and while singing she looks out, over Angelika conducting and silently mouthing the words of *Oh Haupt voll Blut und Wunden* (O Sacred Head, Now Wounded). She looks at the sick and emaciated former soldiers sitting upright in their bunks and the groups of male and female prisoners in padded clothing and Wehrmacht coats right next to the guards and officers in their brown tunics, and her emotions swing between hope and despair. She enjoys the moment, not being hungry and doing something other than working and sleeping, but has to blank out the fact that they are still prisoners who might be forced to stay in the Soviet Union indefinitely.

In September, the first snow starts to fall.

Some of the male prisoners had to wait another seven years before they were allowed to return home, especially if they had been found guilty of a political crime and received 'official' verdicts. In 1955, two years after Stalin died and when West Germany officially became a member of Nato, the Soviet leadership invited West German Chancellor Konrad Adenauer to Moscow for talks about opening diplomatic relations. After consultations with the western Allies, Adenauer accepted this invitation, and in numerous talks and negotiations an agreement was finally reached: diplomatic relations would be established, and in return the Soviets promised that all German POWs and interned civilians still held in the Soviet Union would be released. The last prisoners returned in 1956, more than ten years after the end of the war.

Cilly was luckier, after a fashion. There had been constant promises by Ivan, who followed the brigade to Revda, to her and the other women that each would be able to return if they 'fulfilled the quota'. Keeping prisoners on edge about their potential release was an established 'motivational' technique in the Gulag and Gupvi system – as Cilly learned from other inmates in Revda, there had been instances when other women were told to pack their things and get 'ready to return', when they were just transported to another camp. But as the female prisoners had not been taken as political prisoners and were instead forced labour, the Soviet Union sent most of them home between 1948 and 1949, which helped to bolster the workforce in the newly created GDR. And so the name of my grandmother finally ended up on a list for a transport home.

One day, in October, when Cilly and the others return to camp and march into the yard, she sees groups of women standing together and discussing something very excitedly. What might have happened? Angelika comes towards her, smiling all over.

'What happened?' Cilly asks.

'Cilly, we are going home!' she announces. Cilly doesn't know what to think – she has heard that sentence so often that she just responds: 'Ah come on, you know it's not true.'

'This time it's true! Else from the kitchen overheard the camp commander talking to Moscow on the phone when she was bringing him his lunch. Can you believe it?'

Cilly stares at her for a moment and then lets out a cry of joy and hugs Angelika and two other women standing nearby. 'This is incredible!'

They are all feverishly waiting for the evening roll call, something she would have never thought possible. The women are so excited; they almost cannot cook their potatoes and net-tles because of their shaking hands. It is just unbelievable. There! The bell calls all of them to roll call, and the women just stream from the barracks, all smiles and cheers. They stand to attention amidst the dust their running has stirred up in front of the commander, who stands there smiling and with legs apart. He waits for a moment or two, and then announces: 'Children, you are going home!'

They cheer and shout and cry and hug each other, jumping up and down like little girls, and tears of joy are just streaming down their cheeks. Cilly looks at Angelika and thinks: she looks old now, with the baggy soldier's uniform three sizes too big for her, her long grey braids hidden under the big quilted cap, with only her face visible. The dirt emphasises the wrin-kles around her eyes, and it's hard to tell where dirt and dust end and the dark patches under her eyes begin. Her face is gaunt, the sharp cheekbones stretching the skin. She is beauti-ful. Men must have followed her like dogs the butcher's van in her youth. And while she is tired, as tired as everyone else here, looking at her sometimes gives Cilly strength. Angelika is older than most of them, but where other women cry and moan and pray to God to end their misery, she never says a word.

12 October 1949. Like every morning, the prisoners leave the camp and march to work. Angelika is really jolly, because

the weather is very nice and sunny and she imagines her journey back to East Prussia all the time. She sings hymns on the way to work and seems unable to calm down. Cilly says to her: 'Angelika, don't sing so much – if one is that happy in the morning, nothing pleasant can follow during the day.'

'Ach, what can happen to us? We're all going home soon anyway!'

But Angelika does not go home. From that moment on she has about half an hour to live. The prisoners always have to sit on the open train wagons loaded with wires, iron sheets and old tools. Once they reach the work area at the outskirts of town, they jump down from the moving train. This is not really difficult, as the train is never going fast. So they jump from the train once they reach the forest as usual, but then it happens: Angelika's old Red Army coat gets stuck on a long piece of iron sticking out from the wagon, and suddenly she is dangling head first from the side of the wagon. Before anyone can react or even cry out to the driver, the coat rips. Angelika falls under the wheels, and is decapitated instantly. It all happens so fast, Cilly just stands there and stares at the blood and the limp body. It takes her a while to realise what has happened – Angelika had been singing just a moment ago.

Cilly has seen so many people die and has usually been able to blank out the misery, but now she sinks down on her knees and starts to wail and pray at the same time, screaming out her pain at Russia and the Lord and the Fate that made her give so much time and so many tears to this faraway land that has now taken her only friend. Bettina and another woman kneel down next to her and put their hands on her shoulders, crying with her until the guards come over, raise them up and start cleaning the scene of the accident. Even they seem shocked by what has happened, as if this one unnecessary horrible death is more devastating than all the deaths from war and hunger they had seen before.

The women start to dig a grave, while another woman runs

back to the camp to get the commanding officer and the doctor. When both arrive, they lay Angelika to rest, just an hour
after her accident. Her body is still warm. And while they are
filling the grave they sing, sobbing, hymns like *Where Does the
Soul Find Home, Find Rest?* and a soldier song, *I Had a Comrade*. Even the guards start to cry. The women then cover Angelika's grave with heavy stones, guarding against the wolves.

The following weeks in Revda are very lonely for Cilly, and
every day she returns to the main camp without her friend.
Nevertheless she still has to work and hope for a quick return
to Germany. Carrying wire spools, barrels, boxes; and doubt is
with them all the time – will the Russians really let them go
when they finish their work on the last day? Later, the women
have to paint their barracks white on the inside and outside,
and their old working clothes are made into huge piles and un-
ceremoniously burned. They then receive new clothes: jackets
and skirts made from the same padded material as their old
working clothes, and also something unseen and unheard of in
the last four years: undershirts, panties and finally new headscarves. Cilly's headscarf is dark brown, the underwear made
from pink cotton. And when they receive 150 roubles each,
Cilly doesn't really know what is happening to her. The guards
tell her the money is handed out because they had no holiday
while they were working. Cilly acts frivolously and goes to the
market to buy a mug filled with thick cream and a small wheat
roll. She is sitting on a bench right next to the market when a
beggar turns up. 'Give me a little piece!' she demands, and Cilly
sighs and breaks off a piece of bread, dips it into the cream and
hands it to the beggar. But when the next beggar approaches,
she gets up and returns quickly to the safety of the camp, devouring her bread and cream while walking.

The next morning, she packs the few things she has left: a
picture of Angelika that was taken at a photographer's studio
in town just a few weeks back after they had both received their
leave passes, the rucksack that her mother packed for her the

185

day she left the farm, now bleached and torn, a few dry rolls. Then she puts on her new padded coat and sits down on her bunk, waiting for the roll call. She is ready.

~

I put on my last good black shirt, and wear Cilly's crucifix around my neck underneath it. I'm not religious; but this is the one small thing she brought from East Prussia to Russia and then on to West Germany, the only tangible artefact that made the same journey as Cilly and I, so it is only proper that I wear it on the day I see the places where she spent so much time in the Urals. Maybe I want to give the day special significance, maybe I only want to celebrate my last proper day on Russian soil with the correct attire, I don't know. What I can say is that it feels good to carry something around my neck that she had carried around hers, on trains and fields and in forests and factories.

I shoulder my bag and head down to the lobby: Luba and her friend Sergejy, our driver today, are already waiting for me. Sergejy does not speak English; he's a friendly middle-aged man with brown hair who looks like a businessman, and his car is a large SUV. As we set out from the Iset hotel through the suburbs of Yekaterinburg, past apartment blocks and Ikea and Obi outlets, I tell them how much I'm enjoying being on Russian roads with a native driver and in a large car. My opinion of Russian traffic and road rules is mostly formed by YouTube videos of spectacular accidents involving tanks and drivers brandishing clubs and hatchets and pistols. Luba translates my concerns to Sergejy and they both laugh.

We are soon on the motorway and nearing the village of Kosulino; this is where Cilly spent three years in a kolkhoz in the forest. There is no forest left here today, only fields and bog surrounding a small village. The day is grey and it drizzles and there's a fire somewhere in the bog, filling the air with a not unpleasant tang of smoke. Kosulino has one main road, along which are either old wooden houses or newer ones made from corrugated iron, all built after the same principle. A large, at least 2-metre-high wooden fence encloses a small, one-storey house and what look like one or two smaller sheds. Some are colourful and nicely decorated – we pass one house that is painted with the Olympic rings and the logo of the 1980 Moscow Olympics. We stop near what looks like the village centre, a modern concrete building with a restaurant and a shop. I walk down the main road, over a bridge crossing an overgrown brook and towards the church, the only other modern building in the village. Luba tells me that she made some inquiries, but no one remembers a camp where Germans were kept in or near the village, so we don't even have an indication of where the camp might have been. But I'm content. It feels nice walking around this village where we are the only people on the street, with the smell of burning heather in the air and where every house looks like a small, unthreatening frontier fortress. I scoop up some earth from the churchyard and add it to the earth I collected at the lake in Lengainen. We head back to the car, where Sergejy is waiting for us, smoking a cigarette.

Driving back to Yekaterinburg, we pass a large cross right next to the motorway. 'The memorial to the victims of the Great Terror and prisoners of the Gulag,' Luba says, 'erected over a mass grave that was discovered here.' Yekaterinburg is flourishing and growing: mass graves from the time of Stalin's great purges are still found when new roads and estates are built: 18,000 bodies, 30,000 bodies. The memorial was built in 2002.

The next stop is the town of Revda, where Cilly spent her last months in Russia before being transported back, located on the main road that straddles the Europe–Asia border.

We stop at the border marker between Europe and Asia, just 17 kilometres outside of Yekaterinburg. The monument is small, just a white, metal statue that looks like abandoned scaffolding, on a concrete pedestal with a white line drawn on the ground, separating East and West. In the base of the monument are two stones, one from the extreme west point of Europe, Cape Roca in Portugal, and the other from the extreme east point of Asia, Cape Dezhnev on the Chukchi peninsula. Visitors and newlywed couples, who come here to have their photo taken and drink a glass of champagne, have tied coloured ribbons around the branches and trunks of the trees nearby. It's grey and overcast, the first day of autumn in the Urals and my last full day in Russia, and we're standing next to a motorway built along the road many exiles and prisoners had to walk down when they were sent to the Urals and further on to Siberia, from Czarist times through to the Soviet period. I wonder what they felt when crossing this invisible border. The ribbons are fluttering in the wind, and I'm reminded of the fairy trees in Ireland and Scotland, hawthorn trees adorned with the same kind of ribbons and cloth, places where it is said the passage to the fairy world and the netherworld is closer to the living than in other places. Maybe the same applies in Yekaterinburg.

Like a good tourist I have my picture taken, Luba photographing me standing with one foot in Europe and one foot in Asia, and then we're off.

Revda is a small town with a population of roughly 60,000. It was founded in 1734, next to the river that gives it its name. Approaching it from the east, I finally get to see some mountains – or hills. The area around Kosulino is mostly flat as, like Yekaterinburg, it sits in the stream valley of the Iset. There are some brown hills of 300–500 metres, some covered with trees, others with the colourful summer leftovers of ski slopes. We near the town coming down another hill, past some more wooden frontier houses, and the first image of the city is of one massive factory. Chimney after chimney, giant rusty grey and brown storage buildings connected with a mass of pipes and

wire, train tracks and empty freight cars standing around waiting to be filled; white smoke, grey smoke, black smoke. But this
is not the city proper: behind the factory and around another
bend in the road we reach the centre. Despite the predominant
industry and mining all around, it's surprisingly green, with
plenty of parks along the straight roads of the city. The city was
planned and expanded during the 1930s and grew even more
during World War II, when it was an important part of the
arms industry of Soviet Russia – like the majority of Ural
towns. We stop in what Luba describes as the central city
square – a rectangular concrete square dominated by the ubiquitous Lenin statue and the concrete block of the town hall,
which doubles as a cinema. An almost deserted blow-up fun-
fair is erected under Lenin's blind stone eyes: there's a large
slide in blue and white without cheering children and an
equally deserted miniature quad racing area. If it's deserted because the children are in school or if there aren't any children
left here, I don't know and don't want to ask Luba.

Behind the square is another park, and we walk to a large
statue of a soldier with a Kalashnikov and a worker in black
marble, 3 metres tall and staring defiantly into the distance, the
marble still polished and adorned with flowers. Young couples
stroll around and play in the park under the gaze of these un-
moving giants. The inscription on the base of the statue does
not mention any Gulags or camps, only the brave workers of
Revda.

We decide to have lunch. Right off the square there's a small
cafe with a dining area, with four tables covered in red table-
cloths, and black plastic chairs, all very 1980s. We have a choice
of chicken with potatoes or pork with buckwheat. I go for the
buckwheat, another thing I've grown fond of during my travels. While Luba orders, I study the art on the walls. For some
reason, the owner has printed out random images from the internet and put them on the wall, all nicely framed in light

17 Image of Cilly on a street in the Urals

wood. There are fishes from *Finding Nemo*, a few pictures of penguins, and, strangest of all, a group picture of the cast of *Cheers*.

After lunch, we head back to the motorway again, but I ask Sergejy to stop on the hill overlooking the factory and town. I put my favourite picture of Cilly on the ground and take her picture in front of the panorama of Revda. Just an old photo, in front of brown houses, and white-and-red and grey chimneys and the endless vastness of Russia and Ukraine and Poland and East Germany behind it. It's far from here to Solingen, and I have never been further away from home. It feels good though, now. I'm surrounded by friendly people who are willing to help me and the ghost of my grandmother on our travels; and maybe she and the other women who returned to Germany left something behind here, in the Russian soil and wind and rain.

There is no closure for me, there never was. I knew from

the start where the story would end, and it ends twice: in the sun in Peace Land in 1949 with chocolate smeared around a smiling face; and between 9 and 9.40 a.m. on 17 April 2009, when my grandmother died from the complications of a simple cold. Her death certificate states the town where she was born as Lengainen, Kreis Allenstein. She died in Solingen, 2,000 kilometres from home and 7,000 kilometres from Russia, and she never returned to any of these places.

11 HEIMAT?

The events [...] are distant and strange, but they happened not very long ago, to that woman sitting right in front of me, insisting I take another slice of bread and butter and a fresh cup of tea.

Anna Reid, *Leningrad*

When my grandmother died I wasn't there. To be honest, I was nowhere near in her last two years. I was far from Germany and my mind was occupied with many things, including ending a difficult relationship during that time. After my father moved her to a retirement home, I visited once or twice, maybe. All visits in her final years were highly depressing for me. While I had witnessed the progression of age and the onset of deterioration when she was still living on her own – the rancid yogurt in the fridge and the toilet she often forgot to flush – the sudden change was shocking: the formerly energetic and dominating presence of my stocky grandmother had shrunken to nothingness. Cilly had never before been a frail person, but now she had become this shrivelled husk of a woman, bird-like in her frailty, the skin brittle and too large for the small person inside. Her hair had turned almost completely grey, and her looks were anxious, she was constantly mixing up people and times and was somehow aware that something was not right but could just not say what. A proper conversation was almost impossible. I felt relieved each time I left.

The Cilly who had returned from Russia was not an easy person. For me as a child she was this warm, bubbly granny personality, and I do not remember her raising her voice once when my brothers and I were at her place. She could snub others easily, especially waiters and bus drivers, but I thought that this was a skill all pensioners master at some point. But there was an even darker aspect to her personality, one that I only learned of much later. She was, for example, fiercely protective of my father, her only child, up to a point of misguided jealousy. He brought his first girlfriend home at the age of 14 without telling his parents first. Cilly was cleaning the windows on the ground floor, and when she saw my father walking into the yard hand in hand with his girlfriend, she jumped from the window into the yard, ran over and began slapping him with the cleaning rag without a word. How could he dare to have another woman besides her?

I wonder if she wanted to protect my father, and keep the structure in her life so strong so that she could control it. After all, they had taken her from her first world without warning, and maybe subconsciously she tried to make her second world as strong and fortified as possible. They could come any day, still. After she had seen most of her friends and comrades in Russia vanish into nothingness with all the suffering and hopelessness attached, I don't think she would have been able to bear the loss of my father, however that happened. And so his admiration for another woman was, for Cilly, a step away from her.

She always complained about my mother's cooking to us children when my mother was not there, and could be extremely stubborn if something went against her plans. That longing for security, at least part of it, came from her time in Russia, where they made her wait so long for her return journey.

~

In 1949, while waiting for the train at the station, the released women are forced to camp right next to the tracks in the open.

The guards also search their bundles for contraband, with Cilly wondering what they could have stolen or smuggled from the camp. Before they are allowed to board the train when it arrives, the local Antifa committee first has to decorate it with twigs and red flags proclaiming optimistic paroles. And even after they board and try to make themselves comfortable in the cattle wagon (of course a cattle wagon, but at least a clean one this time), the train still does not move. They have to wait for 50 elderly male civilians from a nearby POW camp. Finally, the next day, they set off. But their journey is not a straightforward one. Sometimes their train sits idling for days on end at forlorn stations in the middle of the Russian nowhere – but their spirits are high and the doors of their carriage are not locked, so with the door open they watch the Russian landscape pass by whenever possible. There is even a kitchen built into one of the wagons, providing them with hot rations. Sometimes carriages are added to their train: wagons with more women from East Prussia and Silesia returning home, and a couple of times they also pass other German POWs on their return journey – there is always a lot of waving and shouting from train to train.

The train they are on also goes for hours without stopping anywhere. Then suddenly it just stops in the open – but they never know how long it will stand there. On these occasions some people make off quickly to do their business. And so it happens one day when Cilly has just crawled to the other side of the tracks to pee that the train starts moving again. As the first wagon rolls past she is really afraid and wonders, what will happen if she is stranded here in the solitude of the steppe. And if someone finds her, will she be sent to another camp again? And for how long? Her thoughts and feelings tumble when she suddenly sees a small footboard at the rear of the wagon that has just rolled past. So she jumps on it and clings to the grab pole above the footboard. She clasps her left arm around the pole while with her right she tries to tidy her clothes through which the cold wind is whistling now.

The train passes through a couple of signal boxes, but unfortunately all signals are on 'go' for their train and it does not stop. Then she sees people. While still desperately clinging to the grab pole, Cilly frantically waves her right arm at some women working on the lines, hoping they will realise her plight and signal to the driver; but they just laugh and wave back at her. It seems to be a normal situation in Russia that women cling to the outside of moving trains. Or maybe they think she is a male worker as her hair is still very short and she is still wearing trousers. After another few minutes she is nearing desperation – beneath her feet the tracks are rushing past, and she sends a prayer to the heavens and tries to hold on to the pole as hard as she can.

This goes on for about two hours, and Cilly is constantly telling herself: 'You need to hold on! And even if the train now goes all the way to the border!' Then finally and to her relief the train slows down and stops. Keeping a close eye on the wheels she crawls under the wagon again to the other side and into her compartment where she sinks onto her mattress, completely exhausted. Her companions had missed her, but just thought that she had been in another wagon. When she tells them her story, they just stare at her.

～

It's my final morning in Russia and the day I'm leaving for Germany. For me it comes after only two weeks in the country, not after four years as it was for Cilly. I am somewhat relieved and sad at the same time. Yekaterinburg has made up for my Moscow frustration, and while it feels OK to leave now, if I had the means and the time I would have stayed longer.

I shoulder my travel bag, which by now mostly consists of dirty laundry and Russian souvenirs, and head down to reception. I pay my bill, crossing my fingers behind my back while the concierge feeds my credit card into the terminal, and wipe invisible sweat from my forehead when the terminal beeps and my bill is printed out. It is cold outside, and the leaves on the trees along the small park in the middle of Lenina Street have started to turn red and brown. I bid a final 'dasvidaniya' to the concierge and the old NKVD building, and walk out to my taxi, which is actually a private car without any markings. But this no longer confuses me in a country where you can wave down any car on the street to take you home. My driver is a young bespectacled Russian in a black bomber jacket who does not speak English, but he knows I'm going to the airport and keeps the volume of Russian techno on the car stereo to manageable levels. The language barrier gives me time to have a final look at Yekaterinburg. Still, the overall impression is grey, but interspersed with some green and brown and red, and I know the streets we are going along and have a rough idea of where I am in time and space, something that has been lacking these last weeks. We pass along the same motorway I had taken the day before, but this time it does not bring me closer to Cilly but to the shiny new airport, where the taxi pulls up right in front of the departure lounge. I shake hands with the driver and shoulder my bags. In the airport hall there's a large model aeroplane formed of empty cigarette packets, seemingly some kind of promotion for a cigarette brand. But again, this is Russia and nothing really surprises me any longer. I buy a *matryoshka* doll for my niece from a shop that, to my surprise, also sells a large array of knives. I have to wait another hour until my check-in desk is announced, and when it opens I'm there almost immediately, the queue moves so fast. At first I don't understand what the young lady behind the desk is saying, so I just say 'To Berlin via Moscow,' with my thick German accent.

She smiles and repeats her question: 'Do you want to sit by the window, sir?'

A riddle wrapped in a mystery inside an enigma, right? It seems as if Russia is trying to make up for the first impression

I had those weeks back. Even the security check is super-fast, I'm placed inside a full body scanner, and I guess that some Russian security guards now know the exact size of my underwear, but again the queue moves at lightning speed and, after a minute or two, I'm sitting at the gate and waiting for my Siberian Airlines flight.

Flying with Russian airlines is to be my final test. Everyone in Germany asked me if I was afraid to fly with Russian airlines, whose planes always seem to disintegrate mid-flight, explode on landing or cannot even lift off because the engineers have run out of duct tape. When I googled the airline for the leg from Yekaterinburg to Moscow Domodedovo, the first thing that popped up was the fact that planes of Siberian Airlines either crashed into the Black Sea after an unexplained mid-air self-destruction or exploded and crashed due to a terrorist bombing. So far so good. But the plane that taxis to my gate is a modern airbus, and there is no difference in the boarding procedure to any other European airport.

There's no turbulence during take-off, and once we clear the grey Yekaterinburg clouds the sun coming through the windows is strong and reminds me that it is still August and summer in other parts of the world. The free in-flight meal is chicken and pasta that I wash down with beer, and I can see the ground below, underneath a few clouds that look like fluffy white sheep hanging in the sky. There's no turbulence on our descent into Moscow Domodedovo either, and after the soft landing and taxiing I'm, for a second, reluctant to leave the plane, I liked the flight that much. I even contemplate returning to Yekaterinburg immediately.

Moscow frustrates me again. Domodedovo airport is hot, loud, hectic, and full of long corridors and crowded plastic restaurants. After the pleasant start in Yekaterinburg I had high hopes of keeping my good mood until I was back in Berlin, but it seems the Russian capital really wants to remind me that I do not like it here. I'm wishing for a calm moment to gather my thoughts before boarding the flight back to Germany, but all the heaving humanity around me makes this impossible. I almost get lost on the way from arrivals back through passport control and to my connecting flight. For a second I wonder if there's any problem with my registration form as the stone-faced border guard keeps inspecting my passport and the form for a very long time, but then he hands it back without comment and I'm on my last Russian metres. Everything is crowded and noisy at the gates: the small gate areas themselves, the Irish pubs, the shops. I had planned to buy some more souvenirs for the rest of my family after getting the *matryoshka* for my niece, but at Domodedovo there are only American and French perfumes and colognes, Scotch whisky and Dutch liqueur. I finally sit down to have beer in a blinking neon-and-plastic internet cafe which is not as crowded as the rest, after which I squeeze into the small gate lounge with many other German tourists and a few Russian businessmen. Thankfully, the Air Berlin plane is a large airbus and I have the three seats in my row just for myself. After a short hold-up we ascend into the blue Moscow sky, and I have a last look at the metropolis on the Moskva. I'm not sad to see it disappear beneath me.

In-flight service is a chicken sandwich and red wine, and as I munch away I realise I might be flying over the Belorussian forests that I passed through, sleeping, over two weeks ago. Before my lunch I was reading a German newspaper that the stewardess handed out, and I wonder if that means I'm returning to reality again, and how Cilly must have felt on the last leg of her journey, through Belorussia and Poland to Frankfurt-Oder in the GDR, before carrying on towards camp Friedland in West Germany.

I'm now covering in five hours the countries and distances it took me over four weeks to get across. In a way, I also tried to make up for 67 years in four weeks, so this speed feels somehow fitting. It's nice to think that in Yekaterinburg people are strolling along the red line and by the lake in the city centre sipping beer, the dancers on the Moskva shore in Gorky Park are lining up for the first square dance of the evening, the small bars off the Royal Route in Warsaw are slowly filling up with patrons, and someone must be sitting in front of the Pozytywka bar in Olsztyn sipping a Warmiak beer and smoking, while the folk music from the amphitheatre washes over the cobblestones and the sun starts its slow descent behind the castle.

I finish my red wine and take a nap. That seems to be the best way to end my journey. I did not sleep that much in the last weeks.

~

Cilly awakes with a start as the train begins to slow down and the locomotive lets out a long howling whistle, announcing their arrival. All around her the chatter has taken up, getting louder and louder. People are craning their heads out of the train windows, trying to catch a glimpse of their location. For hours and hours on end, after they had to change to a passenger train on the new border between the GDR and West Germany, they had driven through the flat white landscape of northern Germany, through the new federal state of Lower Saxony – where their temporary home is located. *Friedland*, Peace Land. Cilly only hopes it will be the last camp in a long line of camps for her: Insterburg, Nizhny Tagil, Revda, a holding camp in Brest-Litowsk and the border camp in Frankfurt. There, they had offered her citizenship in the newly created GDR. It was really just the former Soviet zone of occupation and now a satellite state of the Soviet Union, its roads still lined with Red Army ordnance and Russian soldiers checking her papers, so she said 'No, thank you' to the little grey bespectacled clerk with a clipboard who made the offer and the hulking Russian officer standing at his shoulder. They had just looked at her and gone away.

At least she knows where she is going, from Friedland. Many others on the train do not. In the train are toothless soldiers captured in the battles of Kursk in 1943, prematurely aged by years of abuse and starvation in the Urals, Siberia, Kazakhstan. There are haggard women from camps all over Russia, and even two compartments filled with the sick, still dying after four years in captivity, dying of typhus and pneumonia and malnutrition, sealed off from the 'healthy' passengers. Most of the passengers come from areas that have now been made Polish: Silesia, Pomerania, East Prussia. What Cilly guesses from the few words on the postcards from her mother and has overheard other passengers telling each other is that the Poles have already started to move their own people into houses and farms vacated by their German owners during the horrible days of 1945. Everyone who wants to return to these areas has to become a Pole, on paper at least, relinquishing most aspects of their upbringing and learning, speaking and writing only Polish from then on. Other passengers have news from their families, some now living in makeshift huts in newly erected refugee camps all across Germany, some in houses vacated by other German owners who had fled before bombs and American tanks. Some have no idea what they will be doing after their arrival in Friedland, who might be waiting for them, their families and friends scattered, and some never heard of again. Cilly also knows where she is going next: Solingen. A medium-sized town of 100,000 inhabitants in the newly created state of North Rhine-Westphalia, a town of churches and cottages coated in slate shingles that her brother Otto had visited often during his business travels all across Germany. But first there is the last camp on her list.

~

In September 1945, the Allied Control Commission for Germany built a camp in Friedland, near the American and Soviet

occupation zones. The camp was designed as the first way station for refugees, evacuees and returning soldiers. After being
operated by the British occupation forces, the camp was
handed over to be administered by the newly created federal
state of Lower Saxony in 1947. The camp functioned primarily
as a way station for German (or ethnic German) emigrants
from Eastern bloc countries, especially Poland, Romania and
the Soviet Union. Between 1950 and 1987, approximately 1.4
million people of German extraction came to the Federal Republic from the East; more than 60 per cent of these emigrants
came from Poland. It still serves as a refugee camp today.

Friedland is a sobering place. I visited the camp at the beginning of autumn in the year before my journey. The camp
was much greener than I had expected. There were trees
everywhere, hedges along the streets and football pitches on
the lawns. A large Catholic church in red brick and a smaller
Protestant one made from the same material sat among the
houses and apartment blocks, and the place more resembled a
small provincial town than a refugee camp. Men and women
of all ages were walking on the streets, children playing in the
playgrounds or whizzing about on old rollerblades on the
pavements. It was very quiet. Even the children were not
shouting or laughing, and the adults only talked in hushed
tones, it seemed.

Today the camp is no longer close to a border, sitting on
the northern German plain like a forgotten village. When Cilly
arrived, it was right behind the fault line of the newly erected
Iron Curtain, the first port of call for all the undesirables not
needed for the glorious future of the new socialist republics
springing from the ground everywhere in Eastern Europe. But
today, it does not feel related to any urgency or crisis at all –
despite the fact that the people coming here have always been
refugees. Germans from the East, Hungarians after 1956 and
the failed rising, Chileans fleeing Pinochet, boat people from
Vietnam, Tamils from Sri Lanka, and the most recent are Syr-

ians fleeing the civil war in their country. As I walked along the leafy streets of peace land, I passed buildings from all eras of the camp: wooden sheds and huts erected by British troops, the same that Cilly must have seen, low-lying plastic sheds clearly originating in the '80s and orange three-storey tenement buildings from the '90s. The story of human misery is a long one. I arrived in a small square with a fountain in the middle, and with a large bell sitting in some sort of metal framework standing on a base of red concrete on one side of the square. A yellow cross sat atop the bell. This was the *Friedlandglocke*, donated to the camp by refugees and returning POWs in 1949, as a sign of thankfulness, but its ringing was also intended as a 'reminder of peace and home and a caller for the right of home and self-determination', as the donors stated. The ringing of the bell was broadcast via radio across West Germany when transports with POWs arrived from Russia, and some prisoners were allowed to listen to German broadcasts in their Soviet camps, so the bell rang out into Russia as well. It seems Friedland once had a more prominent place in the consciousness of Germans.

And yet a good story must end to make sense. The ogre is slain, the case is solved. Looking at the downtrodden faces of the people I passed on the streets, I wondered if they were aware that they were part of the story of my grandmother. For their story is hers, and Friedland must look as alien and strange to them as it did to my grandmother. Like Cilly, new refugees are interviewed by the authorities and even the German secret service – for information about the situation in their home countries, for information about comrades that might still be held in captivity or are in danger.

Friedland has a capacity of 1,000 beds, and the refugees here stay for six months while they take mandatory integration courses, where they learn about Germany and appropriate behaviour in the country. Cilly had to do the same: her new country was only a few months old, and although she was born in a republic I doubt that Weimar ideals played a huge part in her upbringing. So she had to learn proper capitalistic behaviour in this new land of Coca-Cola and freedom, I guess. After half a year the refugees from Friedland are sent on to one of the German federal states, where they are housed permanently. Cilly only stayed a day, and I wonder if she was shocked by what she saw here and did not want to linger, or if she wanted her journey to end as soon as possible in her new hometown. But Solingen is part of her second world and I wanted to report from her first, so I'll let it end in Peace Land. It is a good name, after all.

~

Cilly gets hold of a window seat and presses her face against the glass to get a good look at Friedland. The conversations have stopped, and only the clack-clack of the train now tells of their coming. What she sees: to the west there is the red-brick town; to the east there is just open snow-covered fields; and in the middle is the railway line. The station, immediately south of the looming grey-and-brown refugee camp, is unremarkable. It is made of more red bricks and has a red roof. The garden laid out by the side of the station building is also covered in snow, with a few brown stalks poking through, and at the two upper-floor arched windows a neat set of flowery curtains hangs. There is a clock, a noticeboard with a timetable, and a bus stop. Everything is neat and orderly and just as sleepy as it should be. Except today. Today is different for some.

There are several hundred people assembled on the platform and around the station to greet the returnees. Between ten and 20 men and women are carrying signs on which are written details of a missing loved one. One such sign, held by an old bespectacled lady, seems typical of the rest: DO YOU KNOW HIM? UNTERSTURMFÜHRER KLAUS HEINRICH. 1ST SS PANZER DIVISON 'RHEINLAND' & SECOND SS

PANZERKORPS (1943). LAST SEEN AT KURSK, 1943.

Others, maybe less optimistic, are holding little candles and what look like miners' lamps, memorials for those who aren't coming back, Cilly thinks. All this they see from the train, and while the passengers try to remain silent, many start to sob and try to hide their tears. Cilly also sniffs, but she knows no one will be waiting there for her, holding a sign with her name on. She will have to carry on like she has for the last four years: alone. At least for a while. She has a piece of cardboard, a slice of a postcard with the Solingen address of family Maus hidden in her shoe, where it is safest. Then the train slows down and shuffles into the station. The men and women now lean out of the open carriage windows, waving to the people running alongside the track or catching bundles of flowers thrown up into their arms. The train whistles again and halts in the station, and men and women in patched uniforms and stained padded coats stretch out to touch those on the platform amid shouts and cheers. There are calls of 'Get out! All out!' throughout the train, but at the same time soldiers in khaki uniforms without weapons and men in civilian clothes with Red Cross armbands enter the train at the carriage doors and push the passengers back. They raise their hands in apology and announce that they will need to note down the names and places of origin of every single former prisoner on the train before they can disembark. A collective moan goes through the train, but old habits die hard and everyone agrees, especially as the clerks explain that the Russians have not provided any information about who is on the train. Everyone sits down, gazing through the windows and sometimes waving at the people outside, who have stopped throwing flowers and are waiting with anguish and sometimes bated breath.

Cilly's statement taken on the train is short. It merely contains her name and the last Russian camp she was in, Sverdlovsk, Yekaterinburg. It almost seems as if she gave the information hastily, annoyed by this being the umpteenth time she was asked what her name was, where she came from and where she was going.

After almost half an hour, the task is complete and the men and women are finally allowed to disembark. Cilly waits until the majority of passengers have left her carriage, and watches those who have families and friends waiting for them reunite with their loved ones. Only now does she realise how strange and otherworldly her former fellow inmates look compared with the people waiting outside in their Sunday best. So thin are their bodies, so gap-toothed their smiles, so white their hair and so old their weather-beaten faces. Some are filthy and shoeless. Others appear stunned to be in a place that is not filled with cruelty or surrounded by barbed wire and empty steppe. The sick have to be carried from the train on stretchers. On the train, Cilly did not realise that they smelled bad, but

18 Cilly's refugee registration, 1949

then she sees some people instinctively recoiling before the smell wafting from under padded jackets before they embrace their father, son, brother, uncle, cousin, and their sister, mother, daughter, friend. Everyone is smiling, even a few of the POWs, but mostly the former prisoners are crying like stolen children now returned to their aged parents after many years in the dark forest.

~

And then there is this: I don't know what my grandmother looked like in Russia. I know her as a somewhat awkward-looking teenager and young adult, with a too-wide frame and a hooked nose; I know her as the warm and chubby grandmother; I know her as the frail confused scarecrow towards the end. But I could never really visualise her, emaciated and hungry, pushing coal trolleys, felling trees or almost dying in a shed in the woods. Then one day I found the movie section of the *Bundesarchiv*, the national federal archive of Germany, online. The collection includes older documents from Germany's imperial past, Nazi Germany, civilian and military records from East Germany (including East German political parties and mass organisations), and the documents inherited from West Germany's federal archive. Besides the text documents, there are photographs, maps, posters and electronic records. And films. It also keeps films.

My grandmother arrived in Friedland on 20 November 1949. It says so in the top part of her refugee registration form, the one she filled out on the train. When I found out that the film archive of the *Bundesarchiv* was online, I started to search for that date. And I found one movie dating from 22 November, a newsreel intended for cinemas in West Germany – TV had not been introduced to the newly formed German state yet. It is a format called *Welt im Film*, World in Movies. *Welt im Film* newsreels were co-productions of the Allied military governments in West Germany after World War II. Screenings were compulsory to show the films throughout the country. The description for the film I discovered reads:

> Trains from the east. Destination home. Women wave at passing trains. Homecomers leave the train in Moschendorf. A sick man is carried on a stretcher. Homecomers walk toward the camp. Hugs and kisses when reunited with relatives. Homecomer smokes a cigarette. Returning women. Red Cross nurses pack parcels for homecomers without relatives. Woman packs parcel. Registration of homecomers and handout of 90 Deutschmarks. Homecomers put on civil clothing. (57 minutes)

Returning women. I know that this movie was filmed in Moschendorf, another refugee camp for POWs returning from the East, built in Bavaria. But I imagine that the scenes with the returning women might have been filmed in Friedland as well. The narrator, who sounds like he was hired by the Allies straight from the leftovers of Goebbels' propaganda machine with his high nasal tone and invisible exclamation mark at the end of every sentence, says:

> There are also smaller groups of women and girls returning from all parts of Soviet Russia. They are mostly ethnic Germans and East Prussians with the prematurely aged faces of adolescents who suffered a hard fate far away from their childhood home.

Yet all the women are smiling. Their scene is only 16 seconds long, but I keep watching it over and over again. In the first scene men in padded jackets and with Wehrmacht caps help women from a wagon, not a cattle wagon but a proper passenger car. A woman with a headscarf, a padded jacket and a skirt is handed a wooden suitcase and a large clothes bundle. Another woman next to her with a similar outfit, a bulging army rucksack and a clothes bundle turns towards the camera with

207

a quizzical look and then smiles. I'm surprised by how feisty they both look. I had expected a more haggard appearance. But that might be the layers of clothes they wear – there is still snow on the ground. The next scene is a group shot of eight smiling women in front of a fence, a row of barracks in the background. A blonde woman in front wears the padded jacket of Russian prisoners and a fringed scarf. The other women are in uniform and civilian coats, some with headscarves, some without. Their hair looks strangely tidy and coiffed, not at all like hair that has spent three weeks on a train.

There is a woman who might be Cilly. She is standing to the far left, slightly smirking. She has the strong jaw of my grandmother and wears a chequered coat. Her hair looks slightly brighter than Cilly's dark maroon shock of hair. But it could be her, still standing slightly apart from the group, most of her friends dead somewhere in Russia and with the prospect of staying somewhere far from here. She does not need to linger here, in the snow and the camp like the others who will need to stay until someone decides what to do with them. Not her – she needs to keep going, for a short while longer at least, and this is why she is not smiling as much as the others. Like in Russia, she needs to hold back some of her strength and emotions.

～

Cilly steps from the carriage, and someone slaps her shoulder while walking past. She flinches, but gathers herself and walks on. Groups of reunited families and POWs without welcome committees are directed by the Red Cross workers to a longish shed next to the station building. Inside, she shuffles past a long row of tables with clerks behind until she stops at the last but one, where an elderly man writes down her name and address, hands her a piece of paper, two new crisp bills and a chocolate bar, British-made and covered in tinfoil.

'A travel pass and new Deutschmarks,' the clerk says. 'That will get you from here to Solingen if you want to travel on today. But you are more than welcome to rest in one of the barracks. Just follow my colleagues outside!'

Cilly nods and stares at the chocolate. She hasn't seen chocolate for five years. This is a proper chocolate bar, a large rectangular slab of cocoa mixed with fat and sugar and milk, covered in a layer of aluminium foil and then wrapped in printed paper. Maybe it's *Milka* chocolate, the only chocolate brand Cilly ever bought me. Maybe it isn't. Cilly takes it with her.

She steps into the sunshine outside. There's a large patch of grass free from snow nearby, where some of the other POWs are already sitting for an impromptu picnic, despite the cold. Some have bottles of beer and eat sandwiches with their families, others carry cups of coffee and their chocolate from a nearby tea trolley staffed by four elderly civilian women who smile and wave at her. Cilly just shakes her head and sits down in the middle of the lawn, and slowly starts to unwrap the chocolate. First she tries to savour every bite and make it last as long as possible, but then she just breaks off chunks of chocolate and stuffs them into her mouth, smearing her fingers and her face with large brown streaks, like a small girl who was able to steal chocolate from the kitchen and now sits in the barn, devouring the chocolate before one of her older sisters or her mother finds out. The people around her are laughing, she doesn't know if it is about her or not, but she does not care; and even if it started to rain or to snow now she would still keep sitting there on the grass until all of the chocolate had gone. But the sun keeps shining and Cilly munches away until there is no trace of chocolate left. Then she falls asleep.

~

Later, someone will steal ten of the 20 Deutschmarks from her pocket. But whenever she was telling this story, it was important that she was able to eat all the chocolate first before anyone could get it. And after all, this is how I like to think the first world of my grandmother ended: not in frost and misery and despair in Russia, but in the sun, with hope and chocolate smeared around her mouth and on the way to a new home.

12 MEMORYHOUSE

The dead are dead, and it makes no difference to them whether I pay homage to their deeds. But for us, the living, it does mean something. Memory is of no use to the remembered, only to those who remember. We build ourselves with memory and console ourselves with memory.

Laurent Binet, *HHhH*

At some point in the past, I thought, I must have made a mistake and now am in the wrong life.

W.G. Sebald, *Austerlitz*

It's the last time I see her before she moves to the elderly people's home where she will die, but I don't know this yet. Today it's only her and me, which is a rare thing these days. I flew over from Ireland three days earlier to stay with my girlfriend in Solingen, and this is the first time I've visited my grandmother in a year. As I walk up the creaking stairs past the apartment of the Turkish family living on the first floor I smell cooked cabbage, but this time the stairwell is brighter than the one in the house where Cilly used to live with my grandfather. Willy died in 2002, and she is now living in a smaller place across the street from the old house. Still in Solingen, still on Grunewalder Street. If I believed in foresight or karma, the fact that my grandparents lived all their married life on a street named after a forest in Berlin where I am now living might seem prophetic to me. But I don't. Cilly is already waiting at the open door, with an apron over her dark blue dress and in slippers. She is small and somewhat stooped, but her head still has the full shock of maroon hair that I know and remember. She smiles, and as I reach the landing I hug her and plant a wet kiss on her lips. 'Come in, come in.' She keeps smiling and ushers me into the corridor. As I take off my jacket, her words are about food, as always. 'Sit down, the coffee is ready. I have rolls and also bought the good gouda at the supermarket. You would not believe what they charge for cheese these days!'

Her place smells of granny smell; coffee, washing powder and a slight undertone of urine that I ignore. I smile as I hear her shuffling around the kitchen, and after taking off my shoes I sit down at the corner seat of the lounge where I am allowed to sit when my father is not present, and which was always reserved for my grandfather. The table is already laid with two cups and plates and a small basket with rolls, butter, honey, jam. I think about helping her in the kitchen, but I know that she would be mortified and would suss me out immediately, so I stay sat down and allow myself a moment of childish guilt-free granny presence. Her living room is small – she brought the large cupboard over from her old place, the one where the model railway was hidden. The TV in the cupboard is on and way too loud, so I turn down the volume a bit. I hear her talking to herself in the kitchen, and then she brings the small plate with different cheeses and an assortment of cakes she got at the bakery down the road, as she informs me. Cilly cooks like a goddess, but baking cakes and pastry never was her thing. Eating cakes and pastry is. 'Eat, eat!' she says, as she has always done whenever I was sitting at her table. She goes straight away for a piece of marble cake, while I butter half a roll and put a piece of gouda on top. She fills my cup with too-hot and too-strong coffee, and I can add only a drop of cream. I know that it will scald my tongue, as it has always done, but I take a sip nonetheless. She smiles and I keep munching away at the bread in the hope it will cool down my poor mouth. We start to talk,

19 Cilly and Marcel, early 1980s

or rather exchange banalities. I talk about my job and the rain in Ireland and that it rains as much as in Solingen, to which she nods. She talks about how beautiful my girlfriend is, but is she now too young for me? I will come to the same conclusion some time later, but now this is just something I tell my grandmother to make her happy. I am relaxed, I suddenly realise. I don't think about Russia then, and we don't talk about it. That will come later. For now I am just content to sit here, with the TV running in the background, and watch my grandmother eat cake and talk, with crumbs in the corners of her mouth and a slight tremble when she picks up her mug. I feel warm and safe and happy, and I know that I will find at least two open and rancid yoghurts and a brown and wrinkled banana when I open her fridge later, but this is not now.

Cilly was a strong, grown woman when she was taken in 1945, 21 years old. She had had some lovers, or at least one. We know of one at least who was killed in the war – she named my father after him. She had experienced love and despair. Her brothers were gone, killed by the Wehrmacht and the Royal Air Force, her older sisters were with their husbands, so she was the eldest sibling still left at the farm, overseeing the farmhands and all the animals. She had spent over a decade working at her parents' farm, so she knew about the land, the seasons and the work. And she knew how to cook. After she left East Prussia, there was no one to teach her, so she relied on everything she had picked up before. She never cooked anything fancy or extravagant. Thinking of it now, there wasn't much diversity in her cooking, it was just proper granny cooking – filling and with the emphasis on stuffing you properly with comfort food. But it was comfort food prepared to perfection, grounded in East Prussian rural hospitality, the perfect food to induce the first glimpse of the sweet sin of gluttony in us children, leaving us unable to decide between acting out our sugar high or sleeping off our stout and stuffed bellies.

Maybe Russia also had something to do with the fact that she always seemed to fatten up everyone around her, a subconscious need to eat the food available while it was there and to be surprised afterwards that you could always buy new and more foodstuffs. All this blended with that older, ingrained impulse to shower guests with food, equating the level of your hospitality with the amount of calories served. A strange but potent mixture it seems now, rural upbringing and prison camp.

And now I realise: my journey was never about the reasons I imagined. She never wanted to explore Russia (or any foreign lands). She always just wanted to go home, to the fields and storks and lakes. And how strong she must have been, both while in captivity and later, when she knew that world was forever gone.

I would not say that she was as damaged as you might expect after such traumatising experiences. She had her destroyed kidneys and her strange too-strong protective instinct for her only child, but as another witness told me once: there were no psychiatrists for anyone, then. So she lived with it all, and it did not make her a bad woman. And while I rebelled and revolted against my father later, I never revolted against her.

I guess it's just human to try to find a proper ending to a story, to reach the famed 'closure' that seems to be the one thing that ends a traumatic experience. I don't know if such a thing exists. And after all, I forcefully entangled Cilly's story and journey and mine, and tried to make sense of it. But I still cannot say how many of the things she taught me originated in the camps. As my mother and father can testify, Cilly could be a tough woman. Some of her actions later in life were more than questionable – these days, she would be diagnosed with post-traumatic stress disorder. While she could party a lot and be outgoing and generous at parties, she was conservative to the bone and put much emphasis on social status. So many aspects to every human, so many emotions and thoughts and instincts crushing the boundaries of stories and pulverising the attempts to make them into characters. I think that, in later years, when I grew older, I started taking Cilly and my grandfather more seriously than before, when I had been a child. But that is something that happens to most humans. You learn that your grandparents were not always the cuddly, slightly roundish people who always feed you with nice things, that they too are human and have made mistakes and fallen out with people. But is that enough? Even though Cilly always recounted episodes from her travels and the stay in the camps, it was never a full narrative, always missing bits and pieces. Or maybe not missing, but deliberately withheld. And that is fair. I don't think that an eight-year-old should hear about young women dying because their hearts were shrinking as their bodies were using up all bodily fats. Today I can say that I might be able to understand part of what Cilly went through and what must have formed her as a human, but I still find it hard to connect that tough young woman who was raped and almost starved to death with my cuddly, teddy-bear-round granny of later years. But maybe that's the exact definition of the human condition.

In the end, Cilly taught me important things, and most of it when I was little. Enjoy the chocolate bar and the glass of milk while you have it. They might take it from you any time.

It is not possible to come to terms with something that happened in the past, cut it off and lock or hide it somewhere. That does not work. You can only take it and try to form it into a part of yourself, a thing you carry every day and sometimes take out as a reminder and memento. You can't close off the past. It's not even dead yet, to paraphrase William Faulkner. So this is what I tried to do with Cilly's journey and mine. To take it and make it into something that makes me a bit better, remembering her as often as I can. Maybe it's because the one thing I regret about having lived abroad is that I could not help my father care for her in the end. It even felt like a burden sometimes, as if I had spent my benevolence towards her and Willy already and was no longer interested in her suffering. But then again in her head she might have not really suffered. She was confused, yes, but my father told me that she was also mostly living in the past, in the East Prussia of her mind and her soul again. So in a way I try to console myself with this thought: that after a pleasant stay in Solingen she returned to where she had come from, so long ago.

I don't want to spoil my memories of bright red lipstick and wet kisses and strong cuddles, just like I had my glasses of milk and chocolate and chicken soup spoiled by the image of my weak grandmother sitting in an armchair in the old people's home, dried saliva in the corners of her mouth and not recognising me, just benevolently smiling at my father and my mother like they were the children who had brought this stranger to her place. And maybe my father was, in her head, that eight-year-old scallywag again, whom she poured all her love into, thankful that her reproductive organs had not been damaged in Russia. If there's another thing I want to convey through Cilly's story, then maybe it's that I'm glad she made it. There's no god and there's no karma and there's only fate, but she made it, and gave birth to my father and made the best chicken soup in the world, and I'm glad that I knew her once and that she made me part of her world, whether the first or the second one. I miss her.

My favourite picture of Cilly is one that was taken during her time at a health resort after coming to West Germany. At first glance, there's nothing connecting her to the child she was or to the prisoner she was forced to become. And yet it is all there. She is walking with some friends and the picture is taken on a country lane, with an old farm building to the left and a backdrop of trees. There are four women in the picture, but all except Cilly are walking in the background, one cut in half by the frame of the picture. The three women in the back are either looking at Cilly or at their cameras hanging around their necks. Cilly is right in the middle of the picture, captured mid-stride. She's wearing a long bright coat that covers her knees and what looks like a colourful scarf; it looks like an autumn picture. In one hand she carries a brolly and in the other its cover. She's wearing the short perm I've seen her wearing throughout her life, the hair cut short so it barely touches her neck, but covering her head like an explosion of wild black moss, thick and entangled, almost bursting the form her hairdresser had intended it to be confined in. She's laughing out loud, her eyes almost pressed closed by her swelling cheeks, her teeth, all still there after four years of *kasha*, blinking at the photographer. I can hear her laughter, a deep bellowing roar encompassing all her passion and lust for life: for fried chicken cutlets, chocolate bars, her silent husband, swimming in shallow lakes in summer, her son, for being alive.

20　Cilly

TIMELINE

CILLY	WORLD
21 April 1923 Cäcilie 'Cilly' Anna Barabasch born	
	30 January 1933 Adolf Hitler becomes chancellor of the Reich
8 September 1937 Cilly's father Johannes Barabasch dies	
	1 September 1939 Germany invades Poland, World War II begins
	22 June 1941 Germany invades the Soviet Union
	1 August to 2 October 1944 Warsaw Uprising
	13 January 1945 Red Army invades East Prussia
10 February 1945 Cilly captured and sent to Mohrungen	
19 February 1945 Cilly arrives in Heilsberg	
20 February 1945 Cilly arrives at Insterburg camp	
28 February 1945 Cilly transported to Russia	
29 March 1945 Cilly arrives in Nizhny Tagil	
	4 April to 2 May 1945 Battle of Berlin
	1 May 1945 Adolf Hitler commits suicide
	8/9 May 1945 Unconditional surrender of all German forces. Victory in Europe Day

CILLY	WORLD
July 1946 Cilly arrives in Kosulino	1945–7 Famine in Ukraine and large areas of Soviet Union
	24 June 1948 Berlin Blockade begins
1 April 1949 Cilly arrives in Revda	
	12 May 1949 Berlin Blockade ends
	23 May 1949 West Germany founded
	7 October 1949 GDR founded
20 October 1949 Cilly leaves Sverdlovsk	
17 November 1949 Cilly arrives in Frankfurt-Oder	
20 November 1949 Cilly arrives in Friedland	
	15 March 1953 Joseph Stalin dies
1 October 1977 Marcel Krueger born	
17 April 2009 Cäcilie Anna Krüger dies	

BIBLIOGRAPHY

Anonyma, *Eine Frau in Berlin* (Frankfurt, 2003).

Applebaum, Anne, *Gulag: A History* (London, 2004).

—— *Iron Curtain: The Crushing of Eastern Europe 1944–1956* (London, 2012).

Beevor, Antony, *Berlin: The Downfall, 1945* (London, 2003).

Binet, Laurent, *HHhH* (London, 2013).

Budzinski, Robert, *Die Entdeckung Ostpreußens* (Berlin, 1994).

Davies, Norman, *Rising '44: The Battle for Warsaw* (London, 2004).

Donga-Sylvester, Eva (ed.), *Ihr verreckt hier bei ehrlicher Arbeit!* (Graz, 2000).

Dönhoff, Marion Gräfin, *Namen, die keiner mehr nennt* (Hamburg, 2009).

Egremont, Max, *Forgotten Land: Journeys Among the Ghosts of East Prussia* (London, 2011).

Eliot, T.S., *The Waste Land and Other Poems* (London, 2003).

Figes, Orlando, *Just Send Me Word: A True Story of Love and Survival in the Gulag* (London, 2012).

Gaddis, John Lewis, *The Cold War* (London, 2005).

Grossman, Vasily, *A Writer at War*, edited and translated by Anthony Beevor and Luba Vinogrodova (London, 2006).

Grusdas, Rosemarie, *Von Ostpreußen nach Berlin* (Berlin, 1997).

Hastings, Max, *Armageddon: The Battle for Germany 1944–45* (London, 2004).

Karner, Stefan, *Im Archipel GUPVI: Kriegsgefangenschaft und Internierung in der Sowjetunion, 1941–1956* (Munich, 1995)

Kershaw, Ian, *The End: Germany 1944–45* (London, 2011).

Khlebnikov, Velimir, *Russian Poets* (New York, 2009).

Klier, Freya, *Verschleppt ans Ende der Welt* (Frankfurt, 1996).

Kopelev, Lev, *Aufbewahren für alle Zeit!* (Munich, 1979).

Kossert, Andreas, *Ostpreußen: Geschichte einer historischen Landschaft* (Munich, 2014).

Liulevicius, Vejas Gabriel, *The German Myth of the East: 1800 to the Present* (Oxford, 2009).

Loyd, Anthony, *My War Gone By, I Miss It So* (London, 1999).

Orwell, George, *Homage to Catalonia* (London, 1986).

Piechocki, Stanisław, *Magisches Allenstein* (Olsztyn, 2002).

Plath, Sylvia, *The Unabridged Journals of Sylvia Plath* (New York, 2000).

Polian, Pavel, *Against Their Will: The History and Geography of Forced Migrations in the USSR* (Budapest, 2004).

Poolman, Jeremy, *The Road of Bones: A Journey to the Dark Heart of Russia* (London, 2011).

Rauschenbach, Hildegard, *Vergeben ja, Vergessen nie* (Berlin, 2001).

Reid, Anna, Leningrad: *Tragedy of a City under Siege, 1941–44* (London, 2011).

Roth, Joseph, *Das Leben ist ein Wartesaal* (Berlin, 2010).

Sebald, W.G., *Austerlitz* (Frankfurt, 2003).

—— *Die Ringe des Saturn* (Frankfurt, 2011).

Sixsmith, Martin, *Russia* (London, 2011).

Solnit, Rebecca, *Wanderlust: A History of Walking* (London, 2001).

Solzhenitsyn, Alexander, *Der Archipel Gulag* (Frankfurt, 2012).

—— *Ein Tag im Leben des Iwan Denissowitsch* (Frankfurt, 1990).

Steinbeck, John, *A Russian Journal* (Los Angeles, 1948).

Thorwald, Jürgen, *Es begann an der Weichsel* (Klagenfurt, 1949).

Tsvetaeva, Marina, *Russian Poets* (New York, 2009).

Wankowska-Sobiesiak, Joanna, *Agathes Schuhe* (Olsztyn, 2008).

ONLINE SOURCES

Belarsky, Sidor, 'Dark Night', available at www.youtube.com/watch?v=ObzPjTAwvMY

Welt im Film, 22.11.1949, Bundesarchiv Filmarchiv, available at www.filmothek.bundesarchiv.de/video/583666?q=ost-preu%C3%9Fen (accessed 20 November 2014)